LifeFood
Recipe Book

LifeFood Recipe Book

*Living
on
Life
Force*

ANNIE PADDEN JUBB AND DAVID JUBB, PH.D.

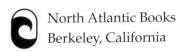
North Atlantic Books
Berkeley, California

Published by
North Atlantic Books
P.O. Box 12327
Berkeley, California 94712

Cover and book design by Jan Camp
Kirlean photographs by Chris Wodtke
Printed in the United States of America

LifeFood Recipe Book is sponsored by the Society for the Study of Native Arts and Sciences, a nonprofit educational corporation whose goals are to develop an educational and crosscultural perspective linking various scientific, social, and artistic fields; to nurture a holistic view of arts, sciences, humanities, and healing; and to publish and distribute literature on the relationship of mind, body, and nature.

The material herein is meant as helpful advice for living a full, healthy life. Remember that all health care professionals are consultants and that you have the first and last word for yourself on your own health. The tissue cleansing diet and flushes outlined here can cause a cleansing reaction and you should read and be aware of the potential effects of this. As always, any program should make sense to you before you adopt it, and only you can decide if something is right for you. The use of good common sense and accountability for one's own health are assumed here.

To contact the authors send letters to: Jubbs Longevity, Inc., 508 East 12th Street, New York City, NY 10009. Phone 212.353.5000.

North Atlantic Books' publications are available through most bookstores. For further information, call 800-337-2665 or visit our website at www.northatlanticbooks.com. Substantial discounts on bulk quantities are available to corporations, professional associations, and other organizations. For details and discount information, contact our special sales department.

ISBN-13: 978-1-55643-459-4

Library of Congress Cataloging-in-Publication Data

Jubb, Annie Padden.
    Lifefood recipe book : living on life force / Annie Padden Jubb and David Jubb.
        p. cm.
    ISBN 1-55643-459-6 (pbk.)
    1. Cookery (Natural foods) 2. Natural foods. I. Jubb, David. II. Title.
    TX741.J82 2003
    641.5'63–dc21

                                                                2003001329
                                                                CIP

4 5 6 7 8 9 10 11 12 13 14 DATA 14 13 12 11 10 09 08 07

ACKNOWLEDGEMENTS

Thank you to our auspicious teachers and exceptional students. This work arose, literally overnight, out of a collective need of our time: to remember nature in our food choices, and to become more natural ourselves.

A warm thank you to my mother, Kathryn Anne Padden, for a lifetime of loving support and for many long days editing our work.

CONTENTS

CONTENTS

CONTENTS

INTRODUCTION

LifeFood nutrition is a diet consisting of fresh raw fruits and vegetables—organic, ripe, and in season; seeds and nuts—sprouted, ground, or whole; and some fermented foods that are properly combined for easy digestion. LifeFood has a radiant, measurable life force field as seen through Kirlean photography. LifeFood does not have a shelf life and will spoil. It should be eaten while it is fresh, or properly dried and stored.

LifeFood is found growing wild in nature all over the earth. More than 95% of all life on earth is vegetation. In LifeFood nutrition we look for fresh wild produce that is teeming with life force and grows well without cultivation. This fresh produce is then artfully prepared for maximum taste and appeal using all modern knowledge with one special twist: to preserve the precious enzymes within the food, nothing is heated above 118°F. Enzymes are the life force of food.

Enzymes break down food. Eat a raw apple and the apples own enzymes break it down for you, and it costs you nothing to digest it. Cook the apple and eat it (devoid of enzymes) and you'll have to beg, borrow, and steal enzymes from your own body: brain, blood, bone, and body tissue. You may feel a little tired afterward, as it cost you light, in the form of enzymes, for digestion to occur. You must borrow from your own precious store of enzymes to digest cooked food. This is the process of aging, the gradual loss of enzymes from the body. In the animal kingdom, when a snake eats a rodent, it is the rodent's stomach enzymes that digest itself for the snake. The snake doesn't have to sacrifice any enzymes from its own body to digest the rodent because everything is there in the rodent. Cook the rodent and feed it to the snake and over time you'll see the life force fade in the snake.

Cooked food makes you sleepy. Witness your own experience, say, after a traditional Thanksgiving meal of all cooked food with barely an enzyme amongst it. How did you feel? Most of us who have been there went into a small hypoglycemic coma to recover. In other words, passed out in the armchair for an hour. What brings you around? "Who wants pie?" You lunge to consciousness to eat even more food, though the stretch receptors in your stomach are stretched to the max. Why? You feel too full and yet can be starving to death on the cellular level for enzyme-rich food that will give you nourishment. This is why, in addition to being addicted to sugary starches, you leap up to have pie even though moments ago you were slumped over in the armchair. Ah, this is the modern American way: too much eating and starvation all in the same body.

There are two ways to discern that you are finished with a meal. One is to be nutritionally complete. In other words, there is a natural shut-off mechanism inside each of us that knows when we are complete with a nutrient. It is called an aliesthetic taste change response. You know for yourself if you have 5 oranges in front of you, you may eat 2 or 3 before you become satiated with that range of nutrients. However, if someone offered you an avocado or a handful of almonds you might go for it, having a desire for a different range of nutrients. The second way of feeling complete with a meal is the worst way: the stretch receptors in your stomach are at their limit and you can't eat another bite. "I'm stuffed," is the usual comment. This is a very poor way to leave the dinner table as you don't feel well and need to rest so that most of the body's processes can focus their effort on digesting, or at least processing, that cooked non-nutritive enzyme-depleted meal. The aliesthetic taste change response only works on whole living food. It doesn't work on de-natured foods, like corn chips and pretzels.

Today, Americans are overweight and obese at an epidemic rate. Some 60% of adults are classified as overweight or obese, and for children the numbers range between 15%[1] nationwide and up to 26%[2] in states like California for children under age 19. Type II diabetes was almost unheard of in children only a few decades ago, while today it is shockingly common. This is in part because corn syrup has replaced sugar cane in all junk food since 1985. (See *The Cornification of America,* p. 35.) Each year obesity claims about 300,000 lives and costs us about $120 billion in health care costs.[3] Cheap fat and corn syrup make it easy for multinational corporations to *Super Size.* The Big Gulp gets larger every year, it seems. What is that stuff, anyway? A half-gallon bucket, a medium size today, of sticky sweet corn syrup beverage with tons of red, blue, and yellow dye. No nutritional value.

We are involved in a Grand Experiment. For the last 25 years some 30% of our diet has been comprised of "new foods." In other words, it wasn't eaten before in all of history; it was instead recently created in a laboratory setting. Think Twinkies, Cheeze Whiz, Skittles, and other non-indigenous edibles. A vegetable or grain is stripped down to nothing nutritionally and then seasoned up with artificial flavors and preservatives, then baked, boiled in oil, or just plain boiled in a way that will give it shelf life. Sometimes out of guilt a product will boast that it is "enriched" as often seen in bread and cereal. Here a grain has all of its vitamins and minerals completely processed out, then pharmaceutical-grade vitamins and minerals are added. This is so the nutrition panel can say anything at all about its nutritional content.

People live a more sedentary lifestyle than ever before. Imagine what the long-term effects will be of eating so many non-nutritive meals and snacks. How much new food in our diet is safe for us, and through our genetics and habits, will be safe for our children? Do we see a strengthening of the overall health of each new generation? Sadly, American children today show twice the rate of weight problems and obesity—some 5.3 million kids—as 20 years ago. Gallbladder disease among children has tripled in the same time period and type II diabetes now afflicts an estimated 300,000 youngsters. This is a ticking time bomb for health care, and something that everyone will have to deal with.

Gratefully, there is much that can be done to rectify the situation through naturalizing your diet with LifeFood nutrition: the freshest perkiest food on the planet. The human body is a perfect self-correcting mechanism. It is a wonder to behold. The most fascinating part is how quickly we regenerate. If I saw you 6 weeks ago and then I saw you again today, there would not be a single cell on your face that was there 6 weeks ago. Each cell has regenerated and new cells are in place. Some organs regenerate at an astounding rate, such as the liver. Half of the liver can be removed and it will regenerate itself in a few short weeks. In fact, there is hardly any part of your body that is more than a year old. Certain bone and dentin in the teeth can be up to 7 years old, but most of the body is much younger than that. However, toxins such as heavy metals, inorganic minerals, insipid pus—such as gallstones and hardened mucus in the sinus passageways—as well as tars, waxes, and resins in places like the liver, and laminations of fecal debris along the length of the intestine, all have much greater longevity than the actual body. In other words, what you are is ever changing and fresh—new. What you are not, the toxins listed above for example, is your history.

It takes about 7 years to form a gallstone. In a 40-year-old, most of the gallstones in the deepest part of the gallbladder are 20–30 years old. This material was formed long ago when the person had much younger ideas about life. We understand that when we eat and digest food we emotionally encrypt that food with how we are feeling and what internal dialogue we are indulging in at the moment. This is why we say a prayer over our food before eating to bless it and to don a spiritual and grateful mood while eating. Let's say that those gallstones were emotionally encrypted with old emotions from a long-ago era—old stuff.

Ancient wisdom tells us that the liver governs the emotion of anger, and the gallbladder governs bitterness. Every person alive has felt something unfair was done to them at some time, and they just didn't deserve it. This is the root of bitterness. One of the side effects of our 14-Day LifeFood Nutritional Fast is a purge of "old stuff" emotions. A common statement will be, "I spent the day rolling through old memories and feeling all the emotions that came with them. What's up with that?"

What's up is that this gentle program loosens years-old debris, allowing it to be flushed out and away along with all the old emotions that were with it. It can be rather shocking what stinky old gunk can come out really quite effortlessly and painlessly during the fast. Old stuff. "Better out than in" is our motto. By safely removing this old material from your body you become startlingly more current in your own life. You stop dragging around your past with you everywhere you go; you are free to live fully in the moment and enjoy it with sharper senses than you had as a child. Mucous deadens the senses, and so much of cooked food is mucous-forming food. Clarity is gained in a short time by liquefying this mucous during the fast. This is a crucial step for freeing ourselves from old behavioral patterns and addictions.

You've never looked so good as you do after our 14-Day LifeFood Nutritional Fast. We flood the body with the purest nutrition, LifeFood nutritional beverages—all rich in electrolytes—naturally flush the body organs of toxins, and watch symptoms alleviate. LifeFood is the ultimate healing diet and the 14-Day LifeFood Nutritional Fast is the fastest way to regain true health. It is turning fully to nature and allowing nature to arise within. Thousands of people over the last 13 years have enjoyed the safe and simple techniques shown here to remove years of debris from the gallbladder and liver. We understand that there is only one disease: toxicity and enervation—a need for more electrical potential on the cellular level. We take a generous approach to health care and flood the body with the nourishment most easily absorbed and utilized. This instantly makes the blood more slippery, and healing begins.

We hope you enjoy this book and use it to create positive changes in your life. Remember, LifeFood is always raw, always alive with enzymes and a measurable life force. LifeFood is teaming with vitamins, minerals, trace elements, amino acids, anti-oxidants, natural medicinal qualities, and other components that the body can easily digest, assimilate, and build high-integrity body parts from. LifeFood can be found growing somewhere in the wild, outside the farmer's fence. LifeFood is vegetarian, congruent with the philosophy that our food choices promote a sustainable future for our planet.

—ANNIE PADDEN JUBB, LOS ANGELES, MAY 2003

LIFE FORCE & FOOD AS MEDICINE

Let your food be your medicine.
—HIPPOCRATES (460–370 BC)

LifeFood is always fresh and alive and has a measurable life force. Foods that are cooked, de-natured by processing, as well as all animal, fish, and fowl flesh, and many other presently eaten foods, are missing life force. What then is LifeFood? And what is life force? Life force is a mysterious and illusive property. It can be detected because it causes things to move, reproduces itself, repairs itself, and produces various effects. For example, an orange photographed with Kirlean field photography reveals electromagnetic lightning storm patterns within and around the orange. This is the life force of the orange made visible by Kirlean field photography. Kirlean field photography depicts the aura, or life force, of any living thing. It photographs the light produced by the life force.

As a food possesses this full-color life force, hues of every shape show up in crystallography and chromium spectrum analysis. Cooked food lacks this life force. Starchy hybridized vegetables possess a much lower vibration than wild-grown vegetables.

Life force is the electric energy a living animal has between its nerves and blood. When the animal is dead, this force is no longer present. Yet, in vegetation, the sun's light (life force) remains within it after it has been harvested. Each cell of the plant stores the energy of the sun within it.

The essential substance from which DNA is built is a proteinacious substance that is a thousand times smaller than any known virus, and causes matter to form from a process called nucleation. This process is the building of life at the cellular level. This formative substance, awash in the saline fluid of our cells, needs to be maintained at a proper acid/alkaline balance. Further, we need to maintain our antioxidant levels and body amplitude of electricity. A strong current of electricity maintains good health. LifeFood is food that gives us spare electrons. Cooked, dead food and even highly hybridized raw food cost us electrons, thus encouraging the process of aging. Be extremely modest with these unnatural foods if you are interested in living a long life!

The root of all disease is toxicity and enervation (low amplitude of electrics in the body at the subatomic level). Detoxify the body, bring back the electricity through LifeFood nutrition, and disease symptoms will alleviate, and vitality be restored. Of course, there are many other factors to a long and healthy life: fresh air and sunshine, cardiovascular and anaerobic exercise, enjoyment of music and art, a sense of usefulness to one's community, a connection to family, and good companionship along with a loving spiritual ethic are important elements to living a high integrity life. The road to vitality is paved with the daily thoughts and actions of the individual. What have you done today that will add an extra day to your life?

A house is a good metaphor for the body. If you were building a house, how many years would you want it to last? Fifty years? One-hundred years? Two-hundred years? To build a house to last for several centuries, you'd be smart to use good materials. You'd make the foundation solid and consider variables such as plumbing, the ventilation system, a septic tank, and so on. You'd put a bit of thought into what you create because you'll live there for many years—perhaps the rest of your life.

It is said that we nearly rebuild the entire body each year. New cells in the blood, bones, brain, and tissue are generated and fresh cells replace the old ones. Some tissue, however, is turned over at a much faster rate. The liver (the hottest organ of the body), for example, is said to be regenerated every 3 weeks or so. Every cell is new and freshly regenerated. Most house dust is actually human skin, an example of the process of regeneration.

LifeFood, enzyme-rich foods, can be completely utilized by the body. An avocado is a rich source of building materials to regenerate blood, bone, brain, and tissue. The enzymes in a raw avocado make it easily digested. Cooked food, heated over 118°F, and de-natured, dead food must "steal" life force and enzymes from the body in order to digest. Because this food is challenging to assimilate, some residue of it will linger in the body, stored along every passageway. The vascular system can become so occluded with plaque build-up that only 10% is open (in angina) for sluggish blood to squirt through.

We are what we eat. Dead food depletes life force in the body, and taps its enzyme reserves to digest it. Dead food makes poor building materials for cellular repair and construction. Eventually, in extreme cases, the body gets to the point where it cannot discern what is self and what is other. It is then that autoimmune diseases can occur. The body cannot discern what needs to be broken down and carried away because it is being maintained with such poor building materials (low amplitude food). Multiple sclerosis is a good example of this where the immune system is trying to deconstruct the body parts because it thinks it isn't itself, but rather a foreign material.

A cooked food diet, deplete of enzymes, does for the body what soggy cardboard would do as structural material for a house. Some say there is more nutrition in the cardboard box than the sugary cereal within. Many people die prematurely due to a leaky gut. The tissue is weak and thin, and the gut ruptures or leaks its contents into the abdominal cavity. The cause of death is often noted as heart failure, which is true, though a leaky gut probably initiated it. A major factor in premature death and disease can be simple malnutrition. Because a person looks well fed, a hospital won't list malnutrition as the cause of death.

Those who are nutritionally sound upon entering a hospital usually show signs of malnutrition and poor blood within 2 weeks on the hospital diet of sugared gelatin, canned meat and vegetables, reconstituted potato flakes, and the like. New York City hospitals outwardly display their nutritional ignorance in the recent trend of replacing hospital cafeterias with Burger King and McDonald's. Sick colon cancer patients must ride hospital elevators with hospital staff, visitors, and other patients holding smelly, steaming bags of greasy fries and burgers while they slurp up sugared empty calorie carbonated beverages.

Cancer patients are rarely given any nutritional recommendations before or after treatment. I saw a film once of 100 post-op cancer patients and not one had been given any nutritional advice at all. It's been true for 30 years that more people are making a living off of cancer than there are dying from it. There are so many wonderful practitioners in this country who are doing their best for health care and their clients, and yet they are completely uneducated about health. Their education is pointed specifically at end point disease and the surgery and drugs that can be applied at that point. There are billions of dollars available for new drugs, yet barely a drop in the bucket goes into researching nutrition. Face it; drugs will never create health in the body. When they get you out of a pinch or through a bad spell, then they are a godsend. However, drugs are not the answer to disease, whether it's physical, emotional, spiritual, or mental.

Many people put more time into the maintenance of their cars than their own body! Buy yourself organic vegetables and eat them. Invest in yourself. LifeFood and exercise are good health insurance for your future. Start planning today to have a healthy life and reach old age, where you can enjoy and be a part of your family. You can ask yourself, "What have I consumed today that will build high integrity blood, bone, brain, and body tissue? What have I done today to add another day to my life?"

ORGANICALLY GROWN PRODUCE

Always seek to obtain fresh, organically grown seasonal produce when possible. Organic produce is grown in accordance with nature and is free of chemical pesticide, herbicide, hormones, genetic tampering, and nitrates. Organically grown food generally has about twice the amount of vitamins and minerals than commercially grown food.[4] Wow! Organic fruits and vegetables contain a high potassium-to-sodium ratio (a good thing), and the organic sodium is biologically available to us and is a good source of sodium. Commercially grown pesticide-poisoned produce contains a higher sodium-to-potassium ratio (a poor thing) with the inorganic sodium being of a poor quality for the body to make any use of.

The differences are astounding: Organic oranges contain 30% more Vitamin C than nonorganic even though they tend to be about half the size. Organic peaches and pears were found to have higher cancer fighting compounds. In fact, a recent review of 41 scientific studies from countries around the world found that organic crops contain on average 27% more Vitamin C, 29.3% more magnesium, 21% more iron, 13.6% more phosphorus, 26% more calcium, 11% more copper, 42% more manganese, 9% more potassium and 15% lower nitrates. Organic crops such as spinach, lettuce, and cabbage show even radically higher nutritional muscle. Organic spinach has twice the calcium, 4 times the magnesium, 3 times the potassium, 69 times the organic sodium, and 117 times the manganese as commercially grown pesticide-laden spinach. Add to that the fact that commercially grown spinach is one of the most chemically sprayed crops in America and organics just keep making common sense.

All organic crops have higher amounts of potassium. Potassium is the major element that facilitates cellular cleansing. Potassium is found in fresh organic fruits and vegetables, and has 19 outer electrons. Potassium is highly heat-unstable. Cooked foods, and inorganic foods, rob us of potassium so that cellular cleansing is hindered.

Chimpanzees at the Copenhagen Zoo surprised their keepers by choosing organic over non-organic fruit when last year they began feeding animals at least 10% organic. Says zookeeper Niels Melchiorsen, "If we give them organic and traditional bananas, they systematically choose organic bananas, which they eat with the skin on. But they peel the traditional bananas before eating them." The choice for organics was a simple one for the monkeys.

We are gatherers by nature. Until recent history we found our food in the wild, brushed it off, and consumed it. Avoid washing home-grown organic produce with powerful cleansers because it will wash away the minute traces of healthy soil that contains Vitamin B12 and other minerals that vegetarians need. Even the invisible traces of spider web and other organic materials help stimulate hydrochloric acid in the stomach! Very important! We are humanizing nature, so we need to become more natural ourselves.

A little-known fact in agriculture is that plants absorb much of their nutrients naturally chelated and in the colloidal state[5] from microorganisms which biologically transmutate[6] minerals from the soil. The vitality of the soil of the earth reflects the health of our own flesh as every natural element found on Earth can be found within our own body.

A superb 20-year study of organic farming conducted by the Swiss found that although organic yields averaged 20% less than those from conventional plots, there was a great saving of resources as the input of fertilizer and energy was reduced by between 34% and 53%, and pesticide use by 97%. In all, organic was far more efficient, producing more for each unit of energy and other inputs they consumed. They also found organic soils to house a larger and more diverse community of organisms, including soil microbes, and mycorrhizae, a root-colonizing fungi that helps plants absorb nutrients. In all, yields were stable over time and soil fertility had dramatically increased.

We cast a vote for our health by the way we live our lives. More powerful perhaps than casting a ballot in any given election year, we are voting each day as we go to the store and make purchases. When you select organically grown produce, you are voting for healthy soil and nutrient-rich produce. Vote for ecologically sound farming practices and clean water in our streams, rivers, and oceans! Vote for the topsoil that your children's children will inherit. Be modest when buying packaged foods. Let your kitchen waste be mostly compost. Pride yourself on making a great contribution to our planet by the choices you make every day. Remember, the organic carrot of 1975 had 10% less lead than today's organic carrot due to air pollution.

THE VIBRANT VEGETARIAN

Vegetarians live longer and healthier than their meat-eating friends do. We'll save you a description of the gruesome and gory current state of affairs in the world of factory-farmed animals, fish, and fowl. Suffice it to say that most of these animals live dreadful lives. Many are diseased and virtually all are loaded with steroids, antibiotics, hormones, pesticides, and/or herbicides. And there is the karmic issue of imposing cruel living conditions on these animals. Anyone spending even 10 minutes in a commercial hen house full of thousands of obviously insane and diseased female chickens would never eat chicken again! Most roosters are killed at birth with an unspeakable disregard for life. Even "free-range" chickens are often raised in crowded pens and infected with salmonella. Vegetarians in the know eat what is easily gathered, and nothing that would struggle to get away.

In parched California more water goes to the cattle than to all human endeavors combined. The water that goes to the cattle is substantially subsidized. It is said that a steak would cost around 60 dollars if the meat and dairy industry had to pay for their water like the rest of us do. There are many cows for each human in America. Cow sewage is not treated and has resulted in fouling up our soil and waterways.

Vegetarians (free of meat, fish, fowl, eggs) live much healthier lives than carnivores.[7] The average meat-eating American will acquire heart disease. The risk of death by heart attack for the average American male is 50%, compared to 15% for the average man who consumes no meat at all. Vegetarian lactating women treat their babies to only 1%–2% of the pesticides in their breast milk than their meat-eating counterparts. The U.S. has some of the highest intake rate of animal protein in the world. It also has some of the highest incidents in the world of colon, breast and prostate cancer, heart disease, and scores of other diseases. In the last 30 years the average American male sperm count has dropped by ⅓! European countries have boycotted our over-drugged animal flesh and many refuse to buy it. In 1994, the U.S. ranked a shameful #40 in the world for newborn infant health—and not much has been done to correct this.

We, as a people, need to do some real housecleaning and straighten up our gene pool. Beggar children in India have been shown to be in *much* better health than our American school kids who are typically fed all the junk food they can stuff into themselves. They tend to be fat, docile, and have dental cavities. Perhaps not surprisingly, 25% of American children are overweight or obese. Americans are the fattest people in the world, and Canadians rank second. How many generations can continue on the current American diet? A large part of this diet was only recently adulterated. Have a look at the ingredients on that package of corn chips, bottled dressing, or microwave dinner— even toothpaste. How many words do you recognize on the label?

When we eat fruit and vegetables they are broken down inside us through the process of fermentation. When flesh is eaten it is broken down inside us through putrification. The average American has 5 pounds of putrifying flesh within their intestine at all times. This sets up an acid condition that is the foundation of many illnesses. At an autopsy it isn't uncommon for 20–30 pounds of fecal debris to be removed from the intestine. Humans have the long intestinal tract of fruitarians, 32-feet long. We are best at breaking down fruit and vegetables. On the other hand, carnivores have much shorter length intestines, 12- to 15-feet long, for rapid transit of their putrifying meal. Again, we can digest flesh, though it isn't really suited to us and all this flesh eating is wreaking havoc upon the delicate life cycles of the planet.

What can one person do? It is said that each person who becomes a vegetarian will personally be responsible for saving a square acre of rain forest. You vote with your lifestyle. Vote with intelligence and compassion for a green planet! Vote for the humane and ethical treatment of animals! Be a living example of the way you want the world around you to be. You are very powerful! Where you spend your money is where industry will grow!

THE LIVING & THE DEAD

Dead, cooked, de-natured food will form an enormous lining of fecal debris in the intestine that is the slow extension of the girth. It will be the slow layering film that becomes cataracts, the shelf of inorganic minerals on the main arteries leading to the heart that eventually becomes angina, the steady packing of gallstones, and so on. This dead food lays the foundation for the physical component of disease mostly from the debris that is left behind from eating it. This creates a great need for real colloidal vitamins and minerals that can be used, through biological transmutation, to build high-integrity body materials. It seems we have a chemist within us that requires a broad range of sub-atomic minerals with which we construct all needed minerals upon demand.

Again, we understand that there is only one source of disease: tox-icity and enervation—the desperate need for electrical activity at the cellular level. All LifeFood has an amazing degree of electrical potential at the cellular level. This electrical potential is seen as light and is vis-ible around all living things—like you, a tree, fruit, or vegetable. It is what animates us and separates the living from the dead.

If you've ever had the honor of attending a person or an animal that is passing on, you may have noticed something amazing. After the final breath, which is a loud exhale, there is a perfect stillness with the dead. When you feel their body you notice a profound change has occurred.

Only a moment before, their limbs were relatively light and supple, where as after death the limbs become heavy and dense. The light, the electrical activity at the cellular level, is gone instantly. The spirit has moved on and is obviously not there anymore. The light that once animated the body is out, gone forever. Human and animal bodies belong to the earth, and while we fill them during life, we leave them behind when we go.

Plants, on the other hand, possess an amazing ability to remain living long after they have been harvested. Their life force light can keep shining long months after harvest. Apples, when properly stored, are sold as fresh a year later. Some plants can retain their life force field and ability to propagate themselves for years in a dormant state. When they discovered King Tut's tomb in Egypt they found perfectly preserved kamut grain, an ancient strain of wheat that had long been a "lost grain" since it hadn't been cultivated in thousands of years. It was in good condition after many thousands of years of proper storage in heshen bags. They added a little water, sprouted it, and it sprung to life—and now you can find it in your local health food store. It has lower gluten than modern hybridized strains of wheat, especially American and Canadian wheat. Plants, through their seed, are designed to last virtually forever, until the time comes for them to spring to life again.

We have the long digestive tracts of fruitarians, and since we are gatherers fruit, vegetables, seeds, nuts, berries, roots, bark, and mushrooms are our natural meals. Grains, legumes, and animal flesh are to keep us from starving to death during lean times. However, they are far from our ideal meals.

STARCH, HYBRIDS, & RUNAWAY SUGAR
(THE GLYCEMIC INDEX)

Many of America's favorite vegetables today have been so highly hybridized that no resemblance of the natural original plant can be found. These hybrid plants have a lower life force than wild plants, and they tend to be very starchy with fast-moving sugars that we'll call "runaway sugars." In fact, we only find starch in hybrids. It is unlikely to find starch growing outside the farmer's fence anywhere wild in nature. LifeFoods have self-protective qualities bestowed through minerals that fortify and protect plants from being overcome by the forces of nature. Those very same qualities that fortify the burdock plant to be able to grow anywhere under most any condition are the very same properties that transfer to you and me when we eat it. Plants growing wild in the fields and forests possess minerals and beneficial electric charges beyond any standard vegetable grown in a cultivated field.

Starch can be found only in hybridized foods. Starch breaks down into carbonic acid in the blood, creating further acidification challenges. Hybridized foods that contain starch enter the liver, along with all the other carbohydrates (sugars), and the liver releases these unnatural sugars (from hybridized foods) much quicker than any other sugars. Sugar from fruit is held onto longer than sugar from rice or potatoes—

both starchy hybrids. Sugars from potatoes, rice, wheat, corn, legumes, and tuberous vegetables cause insulin production to be raised in an adaptive response to those hybridized foods. In this recipe book, wherever we have used a hybrid plant, we carefully balance the recipe with protein and lipids (fats) to help reduce an insulin response.

Much could be said of the woes of having eaten a diet that was full of starch and simple carbohydrates such as pasta, cookies, muffins, bread, noodles, potatoes, rice, and corn products. Insulin has a deleterious effect on the vitality of the body. Wheat, corn, rice, and potatoes can only be found in a farmer's field—not growing in nature.

These hybridized foods are gaining recognition in professional sports as food to stay away from. Today's trainers of the world's top athletes are paying close attention to nutrition to give their athletes the advantage. Starches are mucous-forming foods that leave a fine silt in the bloodstream and in the blood-filtering organs, making blood sluggish and viscous. Athletes, and all of us, should consider these trainers' advice and live like jets, in need of the cleanest burning fuel with the highest octane. It would be silly to put low-octane dirty fuel in a jet, giving it only enough oomph to propel a Volkswagen. It would gunk up the engine in the process and dash the great expectations we have for powerful jets.

In LifeFood nutrition we look for a glycemic index rate of under 50. A rate of over 50 generally requires the production of insulin from the pancreas, which then sets up a whole host of disharmonies in the body. Keeping this in mind will be helpful in remembering the distinction we make between seeds/nuts and grains/legumes. Seeds and nuts, when raw, are LifeFood because they are very low glycemic rate, whereas grains and legumes are very starchy, promote an insulin response, and are only found growing cultivated in a farmer's field rather than wild in nature, and so they are excluded from the LifeFood.

The terms runaway sugars and high glycemic rate foods refer to the rate at which sugar is mediated into the blood by the liver. Low glycemic food, below 50 on the index, is the best and easiest to digest. LifeFood nutrition recipes are low glycemic rate dishes. High glycemic rate food (above 50) is very taxing to the liver and pancreas and is largely responsible for new diseases involving insulin resistance—the constant production of insulin to compensate for way too many starches (fast-moving sugars). The body is forced to produce an enormous amount of insulin to cope with high glycemic foods, and this constantly circulating insulin taxes the body in many ways. We now see several generations of starch eaters and we are finding real genetic degeneration. But how do we build a better human? One mouthful at a time! Lower glycemic rate foods will stabilize the blood sugar levels for extended durations of exercise (greater than one hour) and give you more balanced emotions as an extra boost.

Starchy hybrid foods with runaway sugars include: potatoes, rice, corn, wheat, all grain-flour products, all tuberous vegetables like carrots and beets, commercial bananas, and dates. Other hybrids to avoid, especially by those healing cancer, are commercially grown strawberries, pineapple, mushrooms, kiwi, and soybeans.

Using the Bread Standard Index, where white bread sets the scale at a glycemic rate of 100, here is a brief list of low, medium, and high glycemic rate foods. For a more detailed list we suggest downloading one from the Internet. There are many qualified sites especially ones for diabetics.

LOW GLYCEMIC FOODS (UNDER 50 ON THE GLYCEMIC INDEX)

• All fresh raw non-hybridized fruits and vegetables.

• Fresh raw vegetable juices, all whole fresh raw fruit and vegetables, whole raw nuts and seeds, lightly steamed vegetables

MILDLY GLYCEMIC FOODS
(50–65 ON THE GLYCEMIC INDEX)

- Hybridized fruits and vegetables

- Orange juice and most all pasteurized fruit juices

- Whole cooked grains, such as brown rice

- Dried fruit, like raisins, with seeds and mango, honey, sweet potato, bananas, whole corn on the cob, cane sugar, or popcorn

HIGH GLYCEMIC FOODS
(ABOVE 65 ON THE GLYCEMIC INDEX)

- All de-natured grains and ground grain products

- Rice cakes are the worst offenders—with a glycemic rate nearly off the index at 130!—sure to make a person store fat

- Potatoes—especially white potatoes

- All sugary cereals made from corn and wheat; and most cereals in general, bread, bagels, cake, cookies, pancakes.

- Tofu ice cream at a shocking 160!

- Dates and raisins without seeds

- Carrot and beet juices

NOTE: *The starchy hybrids that have the fastest moving sugars are always in a condensed form, usually with the fiber removed, like in carrot and beet juice. Also, grains that have been ground to a powder (flour) and cooked, such as corn syrup, corn starch, corn meal, and rice syrup. Always apply common sense: munching on a carrot stick is much gentler on the system than whacking back a large carrot juice that may be up to seven carrots. Hybrids are cheap and you will find them at even the simplest of juice bars. The whole food, chewed well, is superior to a de-natured hybrid.*

To avoid hypoglycemic issues (afflicting most everyone today) it's time to switch to a non-hybrid green juice, like my personal all-time favorite: apple, cucumber (or celery), kale, and lemon. This is the most amazing beverage. It is a cleansing beverage and one that I have all of my clients sipping on. It adds energy while gently cleansing the bloodstream and organs. Now, let's be real here, fresh juice is sometimes hard to find—especially when compared to colas and pasteurized corn syrup-sweetened beverages that are available in every store. If the only fresh juice around is carrot, by all means, skip the dead stuff and have carrot juice.

Common sense is king here. I can't tell you how many times I've met someone who boasts that they would never dare eat a banana or a date; however, they eat ice cream every other night. This is pure silliness. Eat a banana and some dates if you're up against a sweet attack and the alternative is ice cream. Then keep plugging away on the green drinks, and they will eventually bring your sweet tooth to a manageable level. Be sensible and have wise discernment.

WHY HYBRIDS?

Hybrids are cheap to produce, can be mono-cropped and picked early, ship well, and can be sold year-round. LifeFood can often be discerned from hybridized plants just by looking at them. Look at any food and ask, "Does this look like it would if I found it growing in nature?" In the berry kingdom, commercially grown blueberries, raspberries, and blackberries generally look about the size and shape, and, when in season taste, as they do when you find them on the brambles and bushes. Now, consider the humble strawberry. I grew up in the San Juan Islands where wild strawberries grow everywhere in the summertime. They were about the size of your little fingernail and so sweet. Today's commercially grown strawberry is treated with a host of modern chemical combinations and endless genetic manipulations. It is the Frankenstein of fruit. It is a giant, nearly palm-sized, compared to its former self. Pumped up to look beautiful like a weight-lifter on steroids, but lacking flavor, hybridized food is often easy to spot and taste. And, of course, strawberries are hardly the worst of the lot. Sometimes it works the other way, like with seedless grapes, which are made to taste unnaturally sweet, they are sprayed several times a week so they will be sterile and are missing the hormones that would be there if the grape were fertile and making seeds.

Hybridized food is often so tasteless (commercial tomatoes, strawberries), so utterly devoid of flavor, it drives the masses to the hyped-up artificial flavors of the fast food and junk food industries (see

Excitotoxins, p. 240). It makes the choice of saying no to the iceberg lettuce salad with hard little tomatoes easy—just having junk food instead.

Sometimes it appears to play out like a conspiracy: The small farmer with high-integrity produce gets squeezed out by the massive farm corporations, the produce gets bland, tasteless, and monotonous, and people stop buying it. The massive farm corporations turn their bland produce into fast food and junk food and sell it at 4 times the price. Sadly, people buy it and become addicted to the hyped-up artificial flavors that white lab coats toil for years to achieve. Chemically addictive flavoring and seasoning are what makes this bland food sell well. How best to sell your product than to have it chemically addictive? "Bet you can't eat just one!" Shamefully, you can't eat just one, because the seasonings are chemically designed to excite your salivatory glands to the extreme. Just like the sleazy drug dealer that smiles when you take your first hit, knowing you'll be back for more, the artificial flavoring and seasoning industries know that if you indeed do eat "just one" you'll be chemically encouraged to eat another, and another, and another.

Looking back in history to the turn of last century, 1900, there were some 63 commercially grown lettuces in California. They were sold locally in the counties where they were grown. Today, there are four primary lettuce types that are commercially grown. They were not selected for their flavor, taste, nutrition, color, or medicinal qualities. They were selected by massive farm corporations for their ability to sell well in far off places. In other words, do they travel well? Iceberg lettuce leaps to mind. That waterlogged bowling ball of a wimpy vegetable.

Of course, all this become possible as a result of the chemical revolution of the 1940s, where huge industry giants like Dow and Dupont came into being with fertilizer sprays for crops, and even for your lawn, to kill, kill, kill unwanted plants and bugs. One horrific example is DDT, which was produced for decades as a pesticide before it was determined that this terrible toxin was inside of us. It was found in startlingly high amounts in breast milk and other places in the body. We absorb whatever we spray on our environment like sponges. At a rate of thousands of gallons per minute, DDT was gassed and sprayed over crops and poor migrant farm workers alike. The migrant workers were concerned when birth defects started showing up, many of them cancerous. They were told it was harmless and a film was released to the public showing children in a field being gassed with DDT by a crop-duster plane, all smiling and squinting through the cloud of chemicals. In the 1970s it *was* found that DDT was responsible for the weak shells that birds of prey were laying. The thin weak shells couldn't hold the developing chick and would break before the chick was mature. Few chicks survived. Countless migrant farm workers babies were born dead or with gross malformations. Hundreds of thousands of eagles, falcons, hawks, and owls were found dead as well, and finally DDT was banned.

In a twist of irony classically seen here in America, DDT was banned *here*; however, as far as I last heard it is still produced in the U.S. and sold to poor developing countries like Chile, where it is used on the bananas that are shipped back for sale in American markets. If it is banned here then it should be banned everywhere, right? DDT is just one example of how big industry chemicals have trashed our soil, poisoned our precious waterways, and created such horrors as a near-extinct American eagle.

This year a remarkable blood study was conducted over a broad range of Americans of every age, race, and economic background; the first of its kind. An alarming consistency of DDT was found in the blood of all the test subjects. All of them.[8]

OUR PRECIOUS TOPSOIL

Ah, but in the early days we didn't worry about DDT and chemical fertilizers, herbicides, fungicides, and nitrates. Or even whether the produce was organic, because *everything* was organically grown. For hundreds of thousands of years everything was organically grown. Even in the last 10,000 years or so of cultivating crops, it is only in the last 60 or so years that we have become so obsessed with chemicals. This goes for medicine as well. For our purposes here, let's begin with the most precious part of soil—the topsoil. Within the mineral matrix of the soil we find a layer so condensed with living colloidal minerals that we dub it the topsoil. It is said that it takes roughly 10,000 years of the life and death cycle to make one inch of topsoil, so it is very precious. I read once that the demise of every great and flourishing culture in past history has been as a result of the unwitting loss of their topsoil through poor land management.

Up until the 1930s we still had most of the topsoil here and the vegetables were radically higher in vitamin/mineral content than vegetables are today. Most everyone had their own garden then, too. With just a little space a beautiful garden could be grown that would feed a family for much of the year. They would grow many different local strains of vegetables, herbs, and fruit in their little garden, and then share the harvest with friends and family. Every community had their own local plants unique to the area, and so a wide range of heirloom plants were cultivated in their gardens. Up until the 1950s more than half of Americans tended their own gardens. Today the number is around 18%. Much of the variety and range of older heirloom seeds have been lost. Massive farm corporations produce a slim selection of fruit and vegetables that travel well: picked green and unripe, shipped to the place of sale, then gas-ripened for sale.

HEIRLOOMS
& THE SPICE OF LIFE

Plants that come from an unadulterated older lineage are called heirloom plants. Variety is the spice of life and so is the amazing range of fruit, vegetables, nuts, and seeds that this land and earth has to offer. Wonderful companies like Seeds of Change[9] are caretakers of the ancient seeds and collect rare high-integrity heirloom seeds to preserve them for future generations. Food is medicine and we need an incredible range of different foods to be healthy.

One of the largest seed banks in the world is the Vavilov Institute of Plant Industry in Russia. It was founded in 1894 and has been meticulously maintained for many decades, housing some of the rarest seeds in the world. A movie was just released that shows how at the end of World War II the dedicated researchers caring for the seed bank chose to starve rather than eat any of the seeds. They put their lives on the line to save this precious resource for food, medicine, and beauty for future generations. Today this seed bank is scrambling for funding to survive. Many seeds stay dormant in freezers and the seed bank is having trouble paying for the electricity. It would be nice to see an international community offer help to secure the seed bank on behalf of the entire human race. We need a wide range of foods to promote health.

The Pygmies in Africa eat a wide range of food. Each week they eat 200 different types of food, and over the course of a year that number totals over 1,050 different types of food. They aren't vegetarian by any stretch of the imagination, though the range of food is astounding. They eat roots, nuts, berries, bugs, fruit, bark, leaves, seeds, beans, vines, tree sap, flowers, grass, eggs from lizards and birds, milk from buffalo and goat, all creatures great and small including *live* monkey, snake, and more—for a total of over 1,050 different foods.

The list of foods eaten in America is startlingly brief. To generalize, Americans eat 2 birds: chicken and turkey; 1 kind of egg: chicken; 2 or 3 animals: mostly cow and pig; one kind of milk: cow; 4 main vegetables: potato, tomato, lettuce, and carrot; 3 fruits: apple, orange, and banana; and 2 grains: wheat and corn. There is an array of seafood eaten in excess, and the oceans are being over-fished; however, the range of nutrition here is very limited, especially when you consider that the vast majority of our food is processed down to nothing nutritionally.

A great deal of this food is then breaded in artificial chemical flavorings and cooked, then sanitarily wrapped in a ton of plastic and paper, frozen for months or years, and then plucked out of the freezer and microwaved; and in 2 minutes it's hot, steaming, and utterly devoid of nutrition to be consumed in front of the TV.

Big industry, having effectively squeezed out the small local farmer, is reaping billions in profits by selling you these packaged foods. I enter one of these massive supermarkets today equipped with a huge cart that I push for half a mile to reach the produce department. I pass 16 aisles of dead de-natured processed foods that have shelf lives of many years. They sit in tins, boxes, plastic bags, plastic bottles, and aluminum cans. Not a single enzyme amongst them. I think of the millions of dollars it took to produce each one of those products. Each product is literally devoid of life. Here lie thousands of empty calories that will form a fine silt of material in the bloodstream and become stored in the arteries and veins, hips, waistlines, and thighs of those who consume them on a regular daily basis.

WILD LIFE

Plants grown wild in nature have a much higher life force field around them than plants cultivated in a garden or field. They fight the daily battle with mold, fungus, yeast, pests, and animals that makes them stronger. What doesn't kill you does make you stronger. For food that has its vital electrical properties intact, consider going to the wildest form of a plant. For example, when choosing between apples, you might want to go for a small tart hard organic Granny Smith rather than a polished waxed huge hybrid Red Delicious with its lame pithy flesh. Always buy heirloom plants and seeds for your own garden, as they are older original seeds that make very high-integrity plants.

Seeds, nuts, flowers, roots, leaves, stems, and bark of wild plants have powerful electrical potential. Many herbs are wildcrafted, grown in the wild and harvested there, and so herbs generally have a very high Kirlean field. Eat plenty of wild foods that have a strong life force, such as burdock root, kale, bok choy, sorrel, heirloom tomatoes, squash, and especially dandelion (leaf, root, and flower).

Dandelions are a favorite food. When dandelions want to grow in a place, say a suburban lawn, it's impossible to discourage them. These plants are very hearty. Juice dandelion leaf and blend it into soups. Find the wild berries in summer, the acorns and pine nuts of autumn, the squashes of early winter, and the new shoots of spring. Take a class and buy a good handbook so you know what to look for. And remember, when foraging for food, make sure that it hasn't been sprayed with pesticide and that it is away from high-traffic roads to avoid heavy metals from car exhaust fumes.

THE CORNIFICATION
OF AMERICA & THE WORLD

Corn is now the most grown crop in America, almost 80 million acres—twice the size of New York State—and the most widely planted cereal crop in the world. Corn is so utterly hybridized that if humans stopped cultivating corn tomorrow it would literally cease to exist. The outer leaves of the ear of corn have been hybridized to be so thick that only a human hand can pull it down and reveal the corn seed inside to propagate itself. If left on its own, corn cannot cast its seed.

Commercially grown corn robs the soil of nitrates and requires more nitrate fertilizer and pesticide than any other crop. It is a very weak plant that Mother Nature would squash like a bug if given the opportunity. I remember as a child hearing a lesson on agriculture where corn was mentioned as being a rotation crop. You would rotate it to other fields so that another crop could revitalize the minerals in the soil because corn robs precious minerals from soil. You simply could only grow it once every four seasons or the soil would perish. This has stuck with me ever since.

A few years ago we were visiting a friend in Illinois. His family grew corn in fields that went on for miles. He was excited to show me his own little patch by the river that his family had given him for his organic garden. We were in a playful mood as we started jogging past tall rows of late summer corn. The tops were well over our heads and my friend jumped through a row and into the cornfield. Not to be outdone we pushed into the cornfield as well and we began running down the narrow rows. Every so often we'd jump over into the next row as we ran toward his little organic patch. I was getting a little winded at this point, and frankly a little creeped out for some reason. I thought of how deep into the cornfield we were, where the rows were so high and seemed to go on forever. I slowed my pace down to a walk and then stood completely still. I looked down at the soil and a very dark feeling came over me. I realized what it was. There wasn't a blade of grass growing out of the soil as far as the eye could see. The only thing growing for acres and acres was corn. I thought, My God, what have they done to the soil so that only corn will grow here?

Of course, not an ear of that corn was destined for a human, directly that is. More than half of the 10 billion bushels of corn produced in America each year are fed to farmed animals for slaughter. Unfortunately, no animal eats corn and therefore cannot digest it properly. It makes them sick, and so their feed is dosed with a virtual cornucopia of drugs, with a heavy accent on antibiotics, hormones, and steroids, to treat the sickness that will surely come from a diet so unnatural to them. Corn is fed to cattle, chickens, and pigs. Now they even feed corn to farm-raised salmon and other farmed fish. None of these animals would eat corn normally, and so virtually all of their feed includes antibiotics to keep them alive long enough for slaughter early in life. Steroids make them grow prematurely large at an early age so they can be slaughtered before showing signs of disease. Chickens, for example, can live in the wild for 17 years, but a factory-farmed chicken is slaughtered at 3 months old—tops. If allowed to live, these chickens would suffocate before their first birthday from the enormous breasts they are chemically designed to grow. Breast meat fetches a higher price on the market (FrankenChickens).

Corn requires a sea of chemicals to grow and tons of nitrate fertilizers and pesticide is hosed all over the earth for the sake of corn. Corn-fed animals retain the nitrate fertilizers and pesticide sprayed on corn. The antibiotics and steroids in the flesh and organs of factory-farmed animals accumulate in the humans who eat them, as well as the chemicals sprayed on the corn. Ah, the Chemical Food Chain in action.

This sea of chemicals wreaks havoc on the environment. Dumped by the ton over the Midwestern corn belt, it washes down to little rivers that drain into the Mississippi River, and then flow out into the Gulf of Mexico where there is now a 12,000 square mile Dead Zone[10] where there is no marine life.

What about us? What effect does all this corn have on the humans that eat it? If corn has trashed our soil, animals, rivers, and oceans and is virtually taking over the world, what is its effect on humans? How well do we do with corn? A traditional Mexican whole corn-based diet, where the corn is visibly and obviously corn, and they just make something with it, seems to be fine. But that's not the case with corn in America. Some 4 billion barrels a year are utterly processed and refined. It is boiled down and condensed and then snuck invisibly into many food products.

Corn is fed to Americans by the gallon as high-fructose corn syrup. Since 1985, virtually all of the cane sugar in junk food was replaced with cheap corn syrup. Corn is an extreme hybrid, with over 10,000 years of cultivation, and its syrup has a very high glycemic rate. Most corn is GMO, genetically modified, for all of its current traits (FrankenFood). It promotes an insulin response, elevates triglyceride levels, and creates hyper/hypoglycemia. Corn syrup is now, and has been for almost 2 decades, the national junk food sweetener. Perhaps white sugar got a bad rap in the vanity of the 1980s and folks felt better if it said corn-something on the label, it seemed like the healthier choice. Not so. Corn syrup can be held up to the light and revealed as a major player in the shocking rise of obesity and diabetes II. Only a few decades ago diabetes II was practically unheard of in children, it was referred to as "adult onset diabetes." Now it is at epidemic rates among our nation's youth.

The rise of corn is parallel to the increase in Type II diabetes and obesity. The most comprehensive study to date in California of 1.2 million schoolchildren found an alarming 26% of kids overweight and nearly 40% not physically fit.[11]

Follow the corn syrup to unravel this mystery. It's in everything: packaged food, fast food, junk food, baby food, juices, soda, sweet tea beverages, canned soup, toothpaste, snack food, cookies, bread, muffins, pasteurized juice, ice cream, and, of course, corn-fed factory-farmed animals (secondary corn). Where sugar was before now there is corn syrup. That's not to say that Americans have cut back on the white stuff; it's quite the opposite in fact, we went from consuming 115 pounds per person in 1970 to 158 pounds per person each year by 1999.[12] However, corn syrup is the dirt cheapest sweetener around and Americans eat more gallons of it each year as it absolutely trashes our health and the environment.

So how come corn syrup is so damn cheap, anyway? The politics at play here are so dark and insidious that it bears scrutiny. Corn costs 3 dollars a bushel (56 pounds) to produce, but the world market is so saturated that it fetches only 2 dollars per bushel. Who kicks in the extra buck to produce corn that the world doesn't need? We do. You and I. The American people kick down that dollar. Why? Good question. Look directly to George W. Bush, who in June of 2002 wrote a $190 billion farm bill. Farm Bill. It sounds so nice, doesn't it? In reality the taxpayers will pay $4 billion per year for the next 10 years to the farmers so they will grow more corn. What? More corn?

Who's getting rich here? Not the farmers. They'll barely scrape by with the farm bill. It seems like the big industry drug-pushers who are producing the chemicals are getting filthy rich here. Corn is born drug-addicted. A sea of chemicals is required to grow this weak frail crop and it requires more pesticide than any other food crop. All those chemicals must be kind of expensive. The chemical soup that is fed to all factory-farmed animals is also pricey. All those antibiotics, hormones, and steroids go right into the corn-based feed. The chemical/pharmaceutical industry fat cats seem to be behind the "farm bill." The farm bill is not for farmers, who will work hard and stay poor, but for rich chemical and drug makers to get richer. Hey, let's be sure to include the oil and gas industries as they're getting richer, too. Corn guzzles fossil fuel to the tune of half a gallon for every bushel. Cheap corn is also making the junk food industry richer, too. I wonder how much money was "contributed" to election campaigns by companies who directly benefited from this bill? Contributed, it's such a nice word for legal bribery, isn't it? This farm bill seems like a transaction between friends, as no one else is really benefiting. America's health is shooting straight down the toilet and the whole farm bill only makes sense to the few people who are getting richer with it.

It doesn't take a rocket scientist to see that this farm bill is just a rigging of the market to create a false future need for corn and therefore all the chemicals, drugs, gas, and oil required to produce it so these industries will be guaranteed a good 10-year run of prosperity. And the junk food industry is guaranteed fat profits from dirt-cheap sweetener that is highly addictive. A nation of corn syrup junkies, fat, toothless, and docile sit staring at the TV, an invention by the way purely designed to market a product. The soap operas were designed to sell soap. Today they will run any show if it will "capture a persons attention" long enough to program (one of the most accurate words in TV) them to buy an advertised product.

Take a stand at the grocery store and stop the hideous cycle of chemically addicted soil, plants, animals, and people. Industry will continue to pollute the environment and health of the people until we literally stop buying it. Our most powerful vote is at the checkout counter. Do the bulk of your shopping in the produce section, and when you do buy packaged food always read the label. What you lay dollars down for today is what will be there tomorrow. Stop buying processed corn products for yourself and your pets and watch the market dry up so we can heal our rivers and bring life to the Dead Zone. Insist on organically produced heirloom foods, free from genetic manipulations so your children can have a healthier life than you do.

Indulge in the lush bounty of nature with the simple and delicious recipes given here. Stock your refrigerator with lots of LifeFood so it's easier to make good choices. Keep a large pitcher of nut milk in there at all times to whip up a quick smoothie or a cream soup, or just for a tall glass with your meal—or instead of a meal. Your energy will perk up and you'll feel better than ever.

THE LIFEFOOD KITCHEN

HIGH-ALKALINE CHARGED WATER

1 gallon distilled water (reverse osmosis, if possible)
8–15 drops seawater (from the ocean!), or a pinch
Celtic sea salt (sun-dried ocean water)
1 or 2 quartz crystals, 3 inches long, or larger
30 drops Alka-Zone (or other alkaline substance)
magnets (optional)

Combine all into a gallon glass jar (a spigot makes for easy access) and cover with a lid. Give the water a good spin to the right and place in a cool place out of direct sunlight, the darker the better. Store in kitchen at room temperature. Use for all water needs, i.e., drinking, recipes, herbal remedies, enemas, etc. If you live inland you can buy seawater at your health food store packaged as Catalina Water brand, or use a pinch of Celtic sea salt (sun-dried ocean water) to re-mineralize your distilled, or reverse osmosis water (see *Minerals,* p. 42). Always store charged water in glass when possible, to avoid the outgassing of plastic (pthyline), which permeates the water.

HIGHLY ALKALINE WATER

Make your charged water more alkaline! The ideal is to purchase a micro-water unit, coral calcium bags, or use a product called Alkaline

Booster by Alkazone (see *Resources,* p. 255, to order). All of these methods will raise the water to a pH of 10 or higher. Highly alkaline water rinses waste from the body at the cellular level. The cell lives an extraordinarily long life, almost appearing to be immortal, when all waste can properly be eliminated from it. Drink 6–8 glasses a day and watch yourself youth.

MINERALS

This water, as well as rainwater, coconut water, and water found in fruit, is free of all ground minerals and sodium, and is pure and clean tasting. Ground minerals tax organs, like the liver and the kidneys. The average liver will filter about 300 pounds of calcium alone in a lifetime!! Drinking charged water takes much of the workload off the liver by reducing the amount of minerals for the liver to filter. We add seawater to repatriate the distilled water with an organic source of minerals and trace minerals. Minerals from seawater are far superior to land sources. This water is easy to assimilate.

This special process of charging water causes it to become highly structured, like lymph. We have 3 times more lymph than blood. Lymph acts like a gas and penetrates through the dentin of teeth and right through the lens of the eye, connective tissue, ligaments, and joints, going where blood cannot go.

CRYSTALS

Adding crystals to charged water enhances the energetic frequency of the water. Charged water can carry a frequency for up to 6 weeks. Make sure your crystals are too large to accidentally swallow! Crystals are found in all radios, as they help send and receive radio and sound waves. The crystals in your water will absorb your energy and broadcast it into the water. This makes the water more structured to your particular frequency, making it more absorbable to you.

MAGNETS

Place a water jar on magnets—any gauss will work. The north side of magnets reduces bacteria and further structures the water. In the same way that magnet therapy reduces inflammation and lowers bacteria counts by placing magnets on the body (north side to body), placing magnets near water make the molecules smaller and more integral. This makes the charged water wetter and more easily absorbed by body cells.

The north side of a magnet reduces and shrinks things, while the south side makes things grow. For our purposes, the north side is preferable. To determine which side is which, put a compass to the magnet. One side will point north, the other will point south. Mark north side with a label. Place the water jar so it sits on the north side.

THE TOOLS OF THE TRADE

Blender
Cutting Board & Sharp Knife
Dehydrator
Food Processor
Juicers
    Fruit & Vegetable Juicers
    Grass Juicers
    Multi-Function Juicers
Nut & Seed Grinder
Shredder
Sprouting Materials
Zester

Blender

A blender is essential for our nutritional fasting program as only blended foods are allowed. Get one that has some power behind it. Shredding and chopping hard vegetables before blending can help the less powerful ones along. The greatest blender is the VitaMix. It is so powerful that it even makes nut and seed butters.

Cutting Board & Sharp Knife

Wooden cutting boards are the very best for hygiene. Plastic cutting boards harbor bacteria even days later. Avoid using a board that flesh has been cut on, especially a plastic board. Keep your cutting board in good shape by occasionally oiling it with linseed oil, every other month or when it looks dry. Sharp knives are essential to the LifeFood chef. Have one knife that you love best for your kitchen and keep it very sharp with a stone or diamond-dust sharpening stone.

Dehydrator

Excalibur is a great brand for dehydrators, but other dehydrators are fine too. They come in different sizes and are simply a box with a fan and a small electric heater in them. They have trays on which to lay food, and will either have open screening for whole food or teflex sheets for wet-blended mixtures. If you have a temperature setting, set it below 118°F to preserve all the vital enzymes in your food.

If you live in a warm sunny place you can sun bake your food to dehydrate it. Screen- or glass-in your dehydrator and set it in a sunny place. Even a cardboard box lined with black plastic can dehydrate food on a hot day. Be creative! Solar dehydration super-charges food better than an electric dehydrator. Give it a try during the summertime.

Food Processor

Any food processor that has an "S" blade and a shredding blade is fine for what you need. I like my CuisinArt, but I also have an old generic brand that works great, too.

Juicers

Fruit & Vegetable Juicers

A simple hand citrus juicer is always good to have. Of the electric juicers, get one that expels the pulp-fiber from itself into a basket. These are best. There are many 40-dollar juicers that can easily get you started. When juicing becomes part of your life you'll naturally want to upgrade. The juicing is more important than the juicer—so just get one and get started!

The Champion juicer is a good workhorse and will last for 20 years, though it is heavy and can be time consuming to clean. Dull grinding wheels need replacing every so often, but parts are easy to find. This juicer is unique in that it will grind up grains, nuts, and seeds. You can

also make lovely sorbets by running frozen fruit through it. Market price is about 225 dollars.

I like the JuiceMan II juicer these days, as it's a powerful and fast machine that is easy to clean. It makes light work of any hard vegetables and is easy to use and store. It will be destroyed in the dishwasher so always hand wash it. It has a vulnerable plastic clip on the top that eventually breaks after a few years. However, I'm brutal on my juicers and always feel I've gotten my money's worth. These will run you about 225 dollars.

The Norwalk juicer is the Rolls Royce of juicers. They cost between 700 and 1,200 dollars and truly produce a superior juice. The hydraulic press squeezes the plant fiber rather than masticating the cell wall, as these other juicers mentioned do. The benefit of this process is that the juice oxidizes at a much slower rate and stays fresh longer.

Grass Juicers

A special juicer is required for soft grasses. A hand-crank grass juicer (about 75 dollars) attaches to your counter and only takes moments to juice any greens for a few ounces of juice. The electric model is just a little fancier and modestly faster and runs for about 150 dollars.

Multi-function Juicers

The Omega Juicer is a superior design to all others, though it's a little slow for large volumes of juicing. The latest unit is all engine, with a handy handle on top and is light and easy to move around. It has two speeds and can be cranked down for grasses. It's easy to clean and comes with containers for juice and pulp. You can make nutbutters and sorbets, too. This design runs for about 300 dollars.

The Green Power juicer is the godfather of all grass juicers. It's big, slow, and heavy—with many parts to assemble and clean, but it juices any greens methodically. This is a wonderful machine that can make large volumes of green juice in a short time. It also juices any other vegetables, fruits, and delicate leaves and grasses. The market value is about 650 dollars.

Nut & Seed Grinder

We like a simple coffee grinder for grinding our seeds down. They are good for some herbs, too. These grinders are cheap and easy to find. They're great for grinding flax seeds to a fine meal.

Shredder

A good hand shredder is essential for people who like to prepare their food without electricity. We love our antique steel single-sided shredder. These are hard to come by, so find one that you like. More common are those that stand upright and have four different shredding options.

Sprouting Materials

Sprouting is made easy with glass gallon or half-gallon Ball jars, or similar style jars. Use a flexible mesh screen (from a hardware store) with a ring lid to secure the mesh tightly. You can soak, rinse, and drain your seeds and nuts in these jars. Other sprouting techniques are sprouting trays for grasses (with or without dirt) and flax or hemp bags that can be filled, the whole bag soaked in water, then hung and drained.

Zester

Zesters are pen-sized hand tools that shreds a single curl of lemon, orange, or lime peel. They make beautiful garnishes and add subtle citrus oils to food dishes. Use the curls fresh, or dry them lightly in the sun or dehydrator, then store in a sealed container in the cupboard.

DEFINITION OF TERMS

Here we list a brief definition of terms used in the recipes and some brand names for living products. More information is provided on important items in Chapter 11, *ABCs of LifeFood Nutrition.*

Raw Apple Cider Vinegar

The only type of vinegar that should be consumed because the body can use malic acid. All other vinegar is toxic to the body because most are pasteurized (making the minerals inorganic) and otherwise contain acetic acid. These inorganic acid minerals deplete alkaloid bases from the body and are less than friendly to the red corpuscles. Several raw apple cider vinegar brands include: Spectrum, Eden, Westbrae Naturals, and Bragg Liquid Aminos. Always keep refrigerated after opening.

Bragg Liquid Aminos

A delicious alternative to soy sauce. Very flavorful with a gravy-like taste with the bonus of containing numerous essential amino acids to supplement the diet. Delicious in sandwiches, soups, and dressings. A staple for any table.

Celtic Sea Salt

This is the ONLY salt that should be consumed. It is most often damp and dirty white to gray in color, and is often sold in bulk at your health food store. It is slowly dried in the sun in a traditional way to preserve marine microorganisms, enzymes, and some 70 minerals and trace elements. True Celtic sea salt is like an elixir, helping heal many conditions on its own. It is very beneficial for our bodies. It helps act like a pump for extra cellular fluid and it is alive, helping impart its good radiation and electricity to the body. It helps digest carbohydrates, proteins, and fats and increases stomach acid.

Magnesium (involved in over 300 detox pathways in the body) is only present when moisture is still in the sea salt. When other sea salt is kiln-dried, magnesium evaporates with the moisture, along with the vast majority of other minerals. This leaves a de-natured sodium chloride salt in its fiery wake, which is a poison to the body. Celtic sea salt, on the other hand, can be biologically transmutated into just about every other element! Bright white salt is usually kiln-dried and dead. Now there are many brands. French Atlantic is a good one.

Dr. Bronner's Mineral Bouillon

Rich condensed flavorful liquid bouillon for seasoning soups, dressings, and other bases. It's found in most health food stores. Use sparingly.

Ferments

Ferments are an amazing food because they provide the body with nutrients that are pre-digested, amino acids—essential fatty acids, simple and complex sugars, vitamins and enzymes, minerals, and many other nutrients. The cabbage beverage, Cabbage and Lemon Elixir, Kombucha, seed yogurts and cheeses, miso, vinegar, Rejuvelac, sauerkraut, chutney, and other various sauces are all ferments.

There are two types of lactic acid: dextrogyral is friendly while levogyral is less than friendly. Unpasteurized ferments have friendly lactic acids as opposed to cooked foods. This friendly lactic acid has many beneficial effects. Apart from keeping the colon slightly acidic at 6.8 pH, dextrogyral lactic acid helps maintain the body's acid base for the blood. This is very important for vitality and healing from cancer and other conditions.

Ferments also contain simple sugars that are bound together in such a way that the enzymes we produce struggle to break down. These simple sugars that are difficult to break down are called fructoolegosaccharides. Fructoolegosaccharides pass directly through our digestive tract and arrive in the colon to feed beneficial bacteria, which include bifidobacterium, lactobacillus, acidophilus, and lactobacillus bulgaricus. Fructoolegosaccharides are fast food for friendly intestinal flora. There are three kinds: fructoolegosaccharides, n-acetylglucosamine, and lactose.

A less than excellent gastrointestinal situation is described as dysbiosis. When you consume fermented foods, however, you will have the most amazing unblemished skin, a vital immune system, a healthy colon, a good disposition, good digestive health, endurance, environmental tolerance, a thin waist, excellent healthy stools, ease during the ovulation cycle, and healthy joints.

Raw Honey

Unfiltered raw honey is loaded with enzymes and is one of the few foods that give us an amalayse enzyme reserve. Honey that comes from a fruit or wildflower source is best because it has sucrose, a beneficial sugar. Honey that comes from a grain is less than excellent. Also be aware that any honey that "pours" can legally be labeled "raw," but has definitely been at least slightly heated. The finest raw honey is found in a more solid form. Be modest with all sugar. Two tablespoons per day is sufficient.

Herbs

— Ground

Peppercorn	Cinnamon
Cumin	Ginger
Coriander	Turmeric
Cayenne pepper	Nutmeg
Cardamom	Curry powder, mild or hot

— Fresh or Dried

Dill	Basil
Thyme	Rosemary
Lemon grass	Sage
Parsley	Cilantro

Lecithin & Flax Seed Meal

Combine these to make a high-density lipoprotein that will draw fat and plaque out of the artery walls and melt cholesterol and generally help with slow metabolism. It is a major ingredient in nerve tissue, semen, and the brain and endocrine glands, as it is used as a precursor to various hormones. It increases the electric tension of the cell membranes making them more permeable to oxygen. Lecithin comes in granules, which are easier to handle.

Unpasteurized Miso

A flavorful paste, rich with protolytic enzymes and micro-organisms. Miso is a concentrated, fermented, salty tasting paste to be used sparingly in sauces and dressings. It has remarkable digestion-promoting properties. Miso is made from soy flower and barley or rice, which is fermented with the aid of aspergillus or oryzae (a fungus). Aspergillus contains highly active enzymes called protolytic that help us digest our food and form immune complements, aiding in the body's ability to breakdown undigested food complexes. It helps strengthen hydrochloric acid in the stomach.

Nutritional Yeast

Technically not a raw food, this is a nutritional and tasty seasoning. Shake onto salads and into soup to add a rich broth-like taste. Yeast has long been used by vegetarians for its rich range of B vitamins, especially B12.

Cold-pressed Oil

Oil Tips: high-quality oil will come in a dark brown glass or opaque hard plastic bottle. Oil packaged in clear glass will oxidize when exposed to light. High-quality, heat-sensitive oil, such as flax, will be sold in the refrigerated section of your food store. Heat-stable oil, like olive and coconut oil, should be stored in a dark cool place. Get organic oil whenever possible and see that the oil has an expiration date.

We are extremely selective about the oil that we ingest. Most oil sold on shelves in stores is rancid and not worth the price paid (to your health) to consume, even if its labeled cold-pressed. Light usually turns most oil rancid when it's packaged in a clear bottle. Most oil behaves much like motor oil in the body. Some good brands are: Omega Nutrition, Flora, Inc., and Life Enhancement Resources. These oils are cold-pressed, organic, and miscible with water!

The Dead Oil Test

Try this—dip your hand in the best oil you can find at the supermarket and try to rinse it off with water. Now try to use soap and scrub it off.

It most likely will still have a small residue. Now try it with live oil—it rinses away with water! This is what occurs in the body. The oil that we consume either rinses away with water or lines the passageways of the body.

If your health food store has yet to carry these fine oils, you can mail order them by writing to:

Flora, Inc.
P.O. Box 950
Lynden, WA 98264

Flora, Inc. is excellent because of their impeccable standards, organic materials, and their wide variety of oils—even exotic ones like pumpkin seed, walnut, sesame, almond, sunflower, safflower, and olive. Another great oil company is Omega Nutrition. We love their garlic and chili flax seed oil, coconut butter, and essential blend oils.

We also recommend the Life Enhancement Resources flax seed oil with borage and use it like a medicine. One to 3 tablespoons a day helps to boost the level of essential fatty acids. Order many or these products from Jubbs Longevity, Inc. at 212-353-5000 (see *Resources*, p. 255). For your convenience, we carry many nutritional and fasting products recommended here. (See Jubbs Information at the back of the book.) Other brand names that are usually found in the refrigerated sections of your

health food store include: Spectrum, Life Enhancement Resources, Omega, and Arrowhead Mills. For more information on oil and essential fatty acids see Chapter 11, *The ABCs of LifeFood Nutrition.*

Rejuvelac

Provides a lactic acid environment for the colon. It is a pre-digested food rich in enzymes and contains aspergillus and helps restore the pH of the colon, which is VERY important to help us digest our food more easily. *Rejuvelac* is good for every member of the family (see recipe, p. 190).

Sea Vegetables

Sea vegetables (seaweed) are 12 times more nutritious than the average vegetable. Sea vegetables are rich in minerals and vital trace minerals—barely found even in the richest organic soil—especially iodine, iron, B6, B12, and magnesium. Iodine helps regulate the metabolism by feeding the thyroid. Eighty percent of our precious topsoil is now in the sea as a result of careless farming practices and overgrazing the land with non-native cattle. Now more than ever we need to supplement our diet with sea vegetables.

Soak sea vegetables in charged water until soft. The soak water is incredibly rich with phytonutrients. Use the soak water in soups or dressing; or give it to your houseplants to appreciate.

Arame: The black angel hair pasta-like seaweed. Soak only a few minutes. It's great tossed into salads, or served as its own dish with chopped or shredded vegetables and sauce.

Dulse: The beautiful burgundy colored seaweed that makes great fast food, it can be eaten straight from the bag. It tears off in layers and melts in your mouth. Keep fresh dulse moist and chewy by storing it in a tightly sealed container. Serve soft dulse in a bowl and add it to your table. Or, when dulse is dry and hard, soak it for only a few minutes, drain, chop it up a bit, and add it to green salads. Use the soak water or the dulse itself for dressing, adding powerful phytonutrients to any meal. Take a bag of soft, chewy dulse with you when you're on the go. When you have it with nuts, like almonds, you have a power-protein snack that will help sustain you when you exercise. A fast food for movers and shakers.

Dulse and kelp are delicious powdered as a seasoning for sand-wiches, salads, or over avocado as a quick snack. You can find dulse and kelp sold powdered, sometimes combined with cayenne or gin-ger, in your health food store.

Kelp: A tough, thick "bull-whip" seaweed usually sold powdered as a condiment.

Kombu: This seaweed resembles green lasagna noodles, long and flat. It is hearty seaweed used in miso soup (see *Mermaid Miso Soup,* p. 61). Soak kombu for several hours until soft.

Hijiki: This seaweed resembles black spaghetti. Soak hijiki for about an hour, sometimes longer, until perfectly soft, drain well. Most good salad bars now feature hijiki salads. Add to chopped or shredded veg-etables and sauce. Keeps firm and refrigerates well.

Nori: Usually sold in sheets for sushi rolls, nori is nutritious, like all seaweeds, and you can roll just about anything in them (see *Sushi Nori Rolls,* p. 98). Smear your favorite pâté on nori sheets to make dehy-drated crackers (see *Cracker Variations,* p. 137).

Shaking Jar

A jar (usually glass) that is easy to hold and has a watertight lid used to mix dressings and sauces. Use instead of a blender for easily blended ingredients.

Shoyu Soy Sauce, Unpasteurized

Monks in Japan make Nama Shoyu for Oshawa brands. We also get this through our health food store in bulk. Use sparingly because of the high sodium content.

Sprouting

Sprouting is the easiest way to have a garden in your own kitchen, whether you live in the country or the wilds of New York City. Use for grass seeds like clover, alfalfa, radish, cabbage, and others. Fill a gallon-sized glass jar with a few cups of charged water. Add 3 tablespoons of the seed of your choice. Cover jar with a wire mesh and secure it with a rubber band. Let the seeds soak for 8 hours to get them going, then drain the water well by placing the jar upside down in the sink for 10 minutes. Put the jar in a dark place (under a towel) for 4–5 days, rinsing 2 or 3 times a day by filling jar with water and draining it well. On the last day, put the jar in the sun and watch the sprouts green up. At that point they are ready to eat. Store in the refrigerator.

Different seeds, legumes, and grains take different amounts of time to sprout. Check it out; it's a lovely energy to have them growing in your home. For grasses, follow the above instructions. For grains, soak them overnight and sprout for 2 days, or until the tail is as long as the grain. For hard peas and legumes, soak overnight and sprout for 5 days. Fine sprouts and sprouting products can be mail-ordered (see www.sprouthouse.com).

Tahini, Raw Sesame

Tahini is a rich paste made from raw (non-roasted) hulled sesame seeds. Most tahini is made from roasted sesame. so read the label carefully. Alyamani and Marantha are good brands that make a raw tahini. It is much more delicious made fresh (see *Raw Sesame Tahini*, p. 152).

Unpasteurized

If a product is labeled unpasteurized it means that the food is probably raw and alive. Pasteurization is the process of heating the life force out of food. Many necessary vitamins and minerals are destroyed by heat. Since the time of Louis Pasteur the world has gone microbe crazy, thinking that the tiny world we find with a microscope is somehow destructive and must be destroyed. This is false. We need this balance of life in balancing our own. Even Pasteur, on his deathbed, said, "The microbe is nothing, the terrain is everything."

CHAPTER 1

SOUP

Soup is nutritious, delicious, and quick to prepare; it is a blended food that is easily digested, and therefore an *ideal* meal for most everyone—especially children, people during a fast, people in any form of recovery, and the elderly. These soups are to be served at room temperature, chilled, or warmed just a bit, **not** cooked (under 118°F), and served in pre-warmed bowls.

LifeFood soup is an important element in the LifeFood nutritional fast program. LifeFood soup is loaded with potassium. Potassium is heat-sensitive and fresh live fruits and vegetables (especially green leafy ones) are the best source for it. These soups have a thousand variations, while each soup has its own unique taste. Substitute vegetables, seasonings, and spices for ones that you have on hand.

SEVENTH HEAVEN SOUP

¼ cup freshly ground sesame seed, or 4 tablespoons raw tahini
½ cucumber, with peel
1 red pepper, cored and deseeded
1 medium tomato
½ cup lemon juice
1 tablespoon ginger root, peeled and chopped
3 whole cloves garlic, peeled
¼ cup red onion, chopped
1 cup cilantro, chopped and loosely packed
½ cup cilantro, chopped and firmly packed
2 heaping tablespoons unpasteurized miso
2 tablespoons Bragg Liquid Aminos or Shoyu soy sauce
4 tablespoons favorite cold-pressed oil, like garlic-chili flax seed or
    olive oil
¼ teaspoon cayenne pepper, to taste (optional)
Celtic sea salt and fresh pepper, to taste
1 heaping tablespoon nutritional yeast
2½ cups charged water

Grind the sesame seed to a moist meal in your grinder; it only takes a few seconds. Cut all vegetables into chunks and put all ingredients together in the blender and blend together. Depending on how much gusto your blender has, you may have to shred harder vegetables, or blend in 2 batches if the vessel is smaller. The measurements fit the Vita-Mix perfectly.

This soup is our favorite to eat! Garnish with Spirulina flakes and a few dashes of garlic-chili flax seed oil, or olive oil. Store sealed in the refrigerator for up to 36 hours. Make some extra tonight for tomorrow's lunch!

Serves 4.

Secret Teaching: Cucumbers contains an enormous range of cell salts that humans deplete through sweat and exposure to sunshine. Muscle cramps are often an indication that these salts need replenishment. Incorporating cucumbers into your meals, whole or juiced, is a great way to top up your natural cell salt reserve!

MERMAID MISO SOUP

4 tablespoons dark miso paste, raw
¼ cake (about 2 ounces) unpasteurized organic tofu
6 cups charged water
1 leaf kombu seaweed, soaked until soft (several hours)
¼ cup green onion or leeks, finely minced

Place all ingredients in a pot over a low heat, stirring regularly. Warm slowly, checking that the temperature doesn't rise above 118°F with your little finger—you'll be able to keep it in the soup comfortably if it's below that. Serve in pre-warmed bowls. Garnish with finely chopped green onion. Serve as an appetizer.

Makes 4 bowls.

SPINACH BISQUE

2 cups organic baby spinach leaves, loosely packed

3 garlic cloves, peeled

¼ cup white sweet onion, chopped in small pieces

2 heaping tablespoons white miso

1–2 tablespoons ginger root, peeled and chopped/pressed

1 heaping tablespoon nutritional yeast

¼ cup hulled sesame seeds (pre-grind if using a regular blender; A VitaMix or stronger blender will them otherwise)

¼ teaspoon Celtic sea salt

¼ cup cold-pressed olive oil

2 parsley sprigs

2 oregano stems

3–5 basil leaves

½ red-hot chili pepper

⅛ cup Bragg Liquid Aminos

½ cucumber, chopped

½ red pepper, cored and chopped

½ tablespoon turmeric powder

1 cup arame seaweed, pre-soaked in 1 cup water for 10 minutes

4 cups charged water

Soak seaweed in water for 10 minutes. Prepare your vegetables and assemble in a blender. Blend on low until entire mixture gets moving, then blend on high until smooth.

This is a hydrating soup, very loose, making it an ideal soup to take on the go with you as you can sip it from a bottle easily. To make the soup more of a meal, prepare bowls with half an avocado mashed or diced finely and 2 tablespoons raw goat cheddar cheese. Pour soup into the bowls and garnish with cayenne powder, spirulina flakes with lecithin, 1 tablespoon garlic chili flax seed oil, and more nutritional

yeast if you like. This makes for a lively presentation and a rich, flavorful, satisfying meal.

Serves 4.

RAVEN'S GREEN HEALING SOUP

1 small whole cucumber
1 lemon, peeled
¼ bunch dandelion greens
2–3 parsley stems
3–4 inches burdock root
2 apples, cored
2 tablespoons cold-pressed olive oil
2 tablespoons spirulina flakes with lecithin
¼ teaspoons gray Celtic sea salt
2 teaspoons powdered Irish moss, or dulse seaweed flakes
2 tablespoons unpasteurized apple cider to blend
1½ tablespoons Bragg Liquid Aminos, or Shoyu soy sauce
¼ teaspoon cumin powder
1 or more heaping tablespoons nutritional yeast
cayenne to taste
3 cups charged water

Blend all ingredients in blender until smooth. This soup is finished best
with generous shakes of nutritional yeast and 1 tablespoon garlic chili
flax seed oil. It is best when blended very smooth. Take it with you for
the day and have your nutritional needs met beautifully. It's an excellent nutritional fast beverage and a vital and nourishing breakfast,
lunch, dinner or snack.

Serves 4.

Secret Teaching: Dandelion is good medicine. It is a wild food that has high electrical potential. This plant has a hearty life force that easily keeps the destructive forces of nature at bay. Teeming with chlorophyll and many important minerals, dandelion is a great way to build up healthy blood.

CURRY CAULIFLOWER SOUP

1 small organic cauliflower, cut into flowerets
1 red pepper
½ avocado, ripe
2 garlic cloves, peeled
¼ cup sweet onion, chopped
¼ cup lemon juice, fresh-squeezed
2 tablespoons raw sesame tahini
2 level tablespoons light miso
3 tablespoons garlic and chili flax seed oil, or olive oil
2 tablespoons curry powder
½ tablespoons turmeric powder
2 tablespoons Dr. Bronner's Liquid Minerals, or Shoyu soy sauce
4 cups charged water, or nut milk

Add all ingredients to blender. Blend on low and then high for a smooth consistency and the result is a beautiful bright soup.

Secret Teaching: Turmeric has amazing antioxidant properties. This is a great soup to take with you when you travel by car or airplane, a time when we are usually immersed in extremely low frequency (ELF) electromagnetic waves. We can all use more anti-oxidants these days, especially city-dwellers, as we live within a sea of ELF electromagnetic waves.

SWEET THAI TOMATO SOUP

1 fragrant young Thai coconut, use water and meat

3 cups Brazil Nut Milk

1 cup baby lettuce mix, loose leaves

½ red bell pepper

2 medium heirloom tomatoes

⅛ cup sweet Maui onion, or Wala Wala sweets

3 garlic cloves, peeled

½ cup cilantro, loosely packed

3 tablespoons Shoyu soy sauce

1 heaping tablespoon raw sesame tahini

3 tablespoons olive oil

¼ teaspoon Celtic sea salt

¼ teaspoon cayenne pepper

fresh ground pepper, to taste

1–2 avocados, diced

Herb leaf, to garnish

Blend all ingredients in a blender. Serve in bowls over diced avocado. Add more salt, cayenne pepper, and ground pepper to taste. Garnish with an herb leaf.

Serves 4.

HEARTY CHILI

2 heaping tablespoons freshly ground sesame seed

1 cup broccoli florets, chopped

1 cucumber, unpeeled

1 tomato

1 red or green pepper, seeded

1–2 sprigs parsley

3 inches ginger root

3 whole garlic cloves, peeled

dash toasted sesame oil

1 small red onion

1 teaspoon cayenne, to taste

2 teaspoons cumin

3 tablespoons Spirulina flakes with lecithin, or blue green algae

good pinch Celtic sea salt

2 level tablespoons unpasteurized miso

4 tablespoons cold-pressed oil

Tobasco hot sauce, to taste

3 cups sprouted quinoa or amaranth grain, or ½ loaf Manna bread (Essene bread)

Grind sesame seed in coffee grinder and put in blender. Chop all vegetables down or shred them. Blend all ingredients, except grain in blender until smooth. Grind grain a bit in a food processor, stir into soup, and warm soup. Garnish with parsley and chopped tomato and onion.

Serves 4.

This soup is delicious in the winter served with extra cayenne and oil! For a delicious Indian-style variation add fresh coriander, dried turmeric, and paprika.

Secret Teaching: Unpasteurized miso is packed full of enzymes. The only comparable source is bee pollen. Miso is readily assimilable as it is a predigested food. This soup is a wonderful appetite and digestive stimulant, and good medicine for the entire digestive tract.

MILLET CHOWDER

2 cups millet or quinoa, sprouted
2 cups water, or *Rejuvelac* (see recipe, p. 190)
1–2 green onion stalks, chopped
2 cups tomato juice, fresh-squeezed
1 avocado, set aside for final step
½ tablespoon powdered kelp to taste
2 level tablespoons miso
¼ teaspoon Celtic sea salt
3 heaping tablespoons freshly ground sesame seed
2 tablespoons vegetable broth powder
young sunflower sprouts
2 cups zucchini, tomato, and mushroom, small cubes spinach leaves,
    chopped for garnish

Liquefy all ingredients except cubed vegetables and avocado in a blender. Stir cubes into blended ingredients. Garnish with finely chopped spinach leaves and short thin slices of avocado (¼ avocado for each bowl).

Makes 4 bowls.

CREAMY TOMATO SOUP

5 medium vine-ripened organic tomatoes

1 green pepper, seeded

1 very small sweet onion

1 large avocado, ripe

2 celery stalks

⅛ cup lemon juice, fresh-squeezed

2 garlic cloves (optional)

½ parsley bunch

¼ cup fresh sweet basil and thyme, loosely packed

½ teaspoon Celtic sea salt

1 heaping tablespoon nutritional yeast

1 tablespoon powdered kelp, to taste

4–6 cups nut milk (Brazil and pine nut combo is good), Rejuvelac, or
plain water

Wash and chop all vegetables and blend well, adding nut milk, *Rejuvelac* (see recipe, p. 190), or water to desired consistency.

Serves 6 cups or 4 bowls.

> *NOTE: tomatoes and peppers are from the nightshade family and should be used sparingly by arthritic persons. See* The Nightshades, *p. 251, for insights on tomatoes and peppers. If you do well with nightshades, a hot red pepper is a nice variation in this soup.*

> *Secret Teaching: Parsley is unusual among plants because it contains an enormous amount of chromium. Chromium helps us cope with sugars, manage weight, and maximize muscle and fitness potential. Chromium is important for the cardiovascular system and cholesterol management.*

WARM ALOHA SOUP

　1 package dried seaweed, about 2 ounces
　2 cups charged water
　1 cake (about 6 ounces) unpasteurized tofu
　2 tablespoons unpasteurized miso, any type
　2 tablespoons ginger, crushed
　½ cup scallions, chopped
　¼ cup lemon juice, fresh-squeezed

Soak seaweed for 15 minutes in the charged water. Put tofu, miso, ginger, hijiki, and soak water in a blender and blend. Stir in the remaining ingredients and warm in a pot over very low heat for a few minutes. Serve warm.

　　Makes 2 bowls.

ISLAND FANTASY SOUP

　1 large avocado
　½ cup burdock root, finely chopped
　1 cup arugula, finely chopped, loosely packed
　2 cups fresh coconut water, or almond milk
　2 tablespoons unpasteurized miso
　¼ cup lemon juice

Blend avocado, burdock root, and arugula in blender. Add in coconut water or almond milk (see recipe, p. 197) and miso. Remove from blender and stir in lemon juice. Serve warm.

　　Makes 2 bowls.

Secret Teaching: Burdock root is a wild food with electric energy. It is one of the few foods containing PABA (para-aminobenzoic acid), essential in maintaining natural hair color and good skin. PABA is very important for blood cell formation, metabolism of proteins, and folic acid production. Burdock root is rich with hormones and minerals. We can all benefit from more of these important nutrients.

EMERALD BROCCOLI SOUP

¼ cup sunflower seed, soaked and rinsed

6 shiitake mushrooms, fresh or dried

⅛ cup Shoyu soy sauce, unpasteurized

1 whole head celery

2 inches ginger root

2 cucumbers

2 whole lemons, peel removed

3 cups broccoli tops, removed from stem

2 tomatoes

2 garlic cloves, peeled

4 tablespoons olive oil

4 tablespoons raw sesame tahini

½ cup red onion

¼ teaspoon cayenne pepper

1 cup charged water

2 cilantro sprigs (stem and leaf)

Presoak sunflower seeds in pure water for half an hour or more. Drain and rinse them. If using dried mushrooms, soak in Shoyu soy sauce with 1 cup of charged water for 1 hour, or until soft. If using fresh mushrooms simply marinade in the Shoyu and a few tablespoons of charged water for an hour.

Remove the mushrooms and set aside for a garnish. Juice together the celery, ginger root, cucumbers, and lemons. Then add the remaining ingredients to the juiced ingredients, including the soy sauce soak water. Blend well. Serve in individual bowls, floating a marinated mushroom in each with a leaf or two of cilantro.

Makes 6 bowls.

Secret Teaching: Onion, garlic, leeks, and chives all contain enzymes that enhance carcinogenic excretion that helps protect against cancer.

GAZPACHO

6 medium tomatoes, chopped well
1 cucumber, peeled and chopped fine
1 small sweet onion, minced
1 green pepper, cored and deseeded
2 garlic cloves, peeled and pressed or minced
1 avocado, or 3 tablespoons flax seed oil
½ cup lemon or lime juice, fresh-squeezed
1 cup charged water
1 jalapeño pepper, deseeded and chopped fine
1 tablespoon Dr. Bronner's Mineral Bouillon
1 tablespoon Bragg Liquid Aminos
½ tablespoon Celtic sea salt
½ cup fresh mix of parsley and cilantro, chopped

Chop all vegetables and place together into a bowl. Blend half the ingredients in a blender to a smooth liquid. Pour the liquefied half over the chunky half and stir together. Serve chilled, garnished with a lemon slice and parsley. Keeps 2 days when sealed in the refrigerator.

Makes 6 appetizers or 4 bowls.

CAULIFLOWER & RED PEPPER SOUP

1 small organic cauliflower, chopped (approximately 2 cups)
1 red pepper, cored and deseeded
1 large cucumber, peeled
1 jalapeño pepper, deseeded and minced
½ cup freshly ground sesame seed
¼ cup cold-pressed oil—coconut, olive, or flax
½ tree-ripened lemon, skin removed, pith in tact
1 avocado
2 heaping tablespoons chickpea miso (or other kind)
1–2 bushy fresh basil or cilantro sprigs
½ teaspoon Celtic sea salt
10 raisins
Charged water to finish, about 4 cups

Put all ingredients in blender and add charged water to fill. Blend well.

Makes 4 bowls.

COOL CUCUMBER-DILL SOUP

3 large cucumbers
4–6 celery stalks (½ a bunch)
½ cup onion, diced
1 avocado
1 red pepper, diced
4 tablespoons flax seed oil
1 heaping tablespoon nutritional yeast
1 tablespoon Bragg Liquid Aminos
¼ cup raw sesame tahini
2 cups charged water
¼ tablespoon Celtic sea salt
1 tablespoon lecithin granules
1 lemon, sliced to garnish
1 bunch fresh dill, chopped

Juice cucumbers and celery. Transfer to blender and add all other ingredients. Put in bowls and float a thin slice of lemon and a stem of fresh dill.

Serves 4.

BUTTERNUT-LEEK FREAK SOUP

    1 small fresh leek
    1 bunch celery
    ½ butternut squash, peeled and deseed
    1 small avocado
    2 tablespoons raw sesame tahini
    4 tablespoons flax seed or olive oil
    1 teaspoon Celtic sea salt
    1 tablespoon maple syrup (optional)
    3 tablespoons chives, chopped
    fresh ground pepper, to taste

This soup is best when butternut squash is in season during the autumn and early to midwinter. Juice the leeks and celery. Shred the squash. Blend juice with all ingredients in blender. Add charged water if a thinner consistency is desired. Garnish with fresh chopped chives.

    Makes 4 bowls.

PEPPER POWER SOUP

    1 each: yellow, red, and green bell pepper
    1 large tomato, ripe
    ½ cup parsley or cilantro (or blend of both), chopped
    ½ cup basil leaves, loosely packed
    ¼ cup onion, chopped
    ½ apple, cored and chopped
    ½ cup freshly ground raw sesame seeds
    2 tablespoons unpasteurized miso
    3 tablespoons raw apple cider vinegar
    ¼ cup Bragg Liquid Aminos, or Shoyu soy sauce
    ½ habanero hot pepper

½ teaspoon salt
black pepper to taste
2 cups charged water

Core and seed the peppers and chop all vegetables. Add all ingredients to blender. Blend well.

Makes 4 bowls.

COCONUT ORGASM SOUP

3 medium organic tomatoes, thinly sliced and halved
½ onion, sliced and chopped
7 ½ cups charged water
1 cup coconut meat, fresh or dry shredded
6 tablespoons miso
1 carrot, finely shredded
5 tablespoons Dr. Bronner's Mineral Boullion
1 zucchini, finely shredded
3–4 tablespoons raw tahini, or ½ cup ground sesame seed
¼ cup dulse, torn into small pieces
3–4 almond or flax seed oil, or coconut butter
¼ teaspoon cayenne powder to taste
raw goat cheese to garnish (optional)

Combine all ingredients in a pot on stove. (Never use aluminum pots.) Use a fork to mash the tomato and onion into the soup to release their flavors. Warm slowly over medium flame for 5–7 minutes. Stir your love into the warming soup. When warm, remove and serve at once. The onion should still be raw and crunchy in the center. For an extra treat, top individual bowls with finely grated raw goat cheese.

Makes 5–6 bowls.

Secret Teaching: This soup is excellent for digestion as it's filled with enzymes and is remarkable for its onion content. Onions are rich in histadine, an important element involved in attaining orgasm.

GARLIC HARVEST SOUP

1 bunch celery

¾ cup lemon juice, fresh-squeezed

3 small or 2 medium tomatoes

1 cup garbanzo beans, sprouted 4 days

½ cup onion, chopped

1 small zucchini

4 garlic cloves, peeled and crushed

1 avocado

½ cup fresh parsley, loosely packed

1 teaspoon paprika

1 teaspoon black pepper

1–2 fresh basil stems with leaves

4 tablespoons raw sesame tahini, or ½ cup ground sesame seed

1 teaspoon dried thyme, or 3 tablespoons fresh

1 tablespoon flax seed oil

3 tablespoons raw apple cider vinegar

¾ cup pumpkin or sunflower seed, soaked for an hour and drained

Juice celery and lemon. Chop all vegetables. Blend juice and other ingredients, reserving half a tomato, in blender and blend well. Float thin slices of tomato cut from reserved tomato into each bowl as a garnish. Add water if a thinner consistency is desired.

Serves 4–6.

Secret Teaching: Garlic gives off ultraviolet rays as mitogenetic radiation called Gurwitch rays. Garlic has miraculous oil called allicin that acts like a steam shovel. Diallyldisulfide is created in the digestive tract from allicin and is involved in initiating a powerful internal cleansing to clear away and reduce lipid levels in the liver and blood.

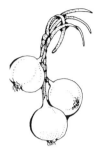

Minerals in onions invigorate the allicin in garlic. Raw apple cider vinegar has high potassium content that boosts allicin's enzymatic activity. Allicin then penetrates the wall of the large intestine, stimulating peristaltic activity and movement of sluggish fecal-covered intestinal walls. The allicin in this dynamic formula helps dislodge accumulated waste.

CHAPTER 2

SALADS & ENTREES

GARDEN SALAD

½ cup raw sunflower seeds, soaked
½ cup raw almonds, soaked
charged water for soaking
3 handfuls romaine lettuce, torn
3 fresh shiitake mushrooms, sliced
1 handful zucchini, grated
4 cucumber slices
3 fat tomato slices
2 scoops avocado
1 handful mung bean sprouts

Soak sunflower seeds and almonds in charged water for about an hour. Drain water and rinse with fresh water. Arrange the salad together attractively. Begin with the romaine lettuce, tearing it into bite-sized pieces. Add mushrooms, zucchini, and other vegetables. Serve with *Zesty Herb Dressing* or *Tahini Tamari Dressing* (see recipes, p. 116).

Makes a hearty meal for 1.

ANNIE'S FAVORITE SALAD

3 leaves each: crunchy romaine and red leaf lettuce
1 branch broccoli
1 handful baby spinach leaves
½ cup each: clover and sunflower sprouts
½ cucumber, sliced into thin rounds
freshly ground pumpkin seeds, to garnish

Tear lettuce into pieces in a large bowl. Run the broccoli branch under very hot tap water for a few moments until it turns a bright green. Hold onto the stem of the broccoli and carefully shave off the ends (florets) over the lettuce. Cut the hard outer bark from the stem on all sides, slice them lengthwise and in half until they are chopstick width. Add broccoli stems, spinach, sprouts, and cucumber to salad. Add sprouts. Toss with *Dill Vinaigrette* (see recipe, p. 116). Grind pumpkin seeds in grinder and sprinkle over salad.

A delicious meal for 1.

GREEK SALAD

small wedge organic feta cheese (unpasteurized)
1 head favorite lettuce (red leaf, romaine, etc.)
3 vine-ripened tomatoes, chopped
1–2 cucumbers, peeled, sliced, and diced
½ red onion, chopped
¼ cup olive oil
¼ cup raw apple cider vinegar

Rinse salt off feta cheese. Tear lettuce into a large festive bowl. Add tomatoes, cucumber, and red onion. Crumble feta over salad. Drizzle with oil and vinegar and toss well to mix the flavors together.

NOTE: The recipe for Greek Salad *is considered a transitional dish (for carnivores becoming vegetarians) because of the feta cheese. We understand the importance of transitional foods and so include this dish, while still encouraging an animal-free diet.*

SEASER SALAD

1 head crispy fresh romaine lettuce
1 package (7 sushi sheets) nori seaweed
½ cup unpasteurized Parmesan cheese, grated
¼ cup cold-pressed olive oil
¼ cup raw apple cider vinegar

Chop the romaine lettuce into bite-sized pieces. Cut the nori sheets with scissors into ½-inch strips, then cut them to 3-inch lengths. Toss all ingredients in a large salad bowl and drizzle with oil and vinegar. Toss again.

This mouth-watering salad serves 4.

HUMMUS

3 cups sprouted chickpeas
½ cup charged water
1 teaspoon kelp powder
1–2 large garlic cloves, peeled and minced
⅛ teaspoon cayenne powder
2 tablespoons olive oil
½ cup tahini
1 tablespoon raw apple cider vinegar
paprika to garnish

Blend the sprouted chickpeas with water in food processor to a paste using the "S" blade. Add other ingredients and blend until smooth. Place in bowl and sprinkle with paprika. Variation: for an eye-catching change, add ½ cup chopped cilantro for a green hummus.

NOTE: Chickpeas are very starchy, even when sprouted. They are not considered to be a LifeFood, but can be enjoyed occasionally.

ARAME CUCUMBER SALAD

1 cup raw almonds
Charged water for soaking
1 package (about 2 ounces) arame sea vegetable
2 cucumbers with peel
1 bunch radishes
1 red pepper, deseeded sliced lengthwise
¼ white onion, chopped
1 cup sunflower seeds
1 small carrot, shredded
Cayenne power, and garlic powder, to taste
Shoyu soy sauce, to taste
¼ cup cold-pressed olive oil
⅛ cup raw apple cider vinegar

Soak almonds and seeds in water for 1 hour. Soak arame seaweed in charged water until soft, about 10 minutes. Drain well. Slice cucumber and radishes diagonally, and the red pepper into long thin lengths. Place all ingredients in a bowl with onion, sunflower seeds, and carrot, and season with cayenne powder and garlic powder. Drizzle oil, vinegar, and soy sauce. Toss well.

Serves 4.

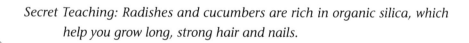

Secret Teaching: Radishes and cucumbers are rich in organic silica, which help you grow long, strong hair and nails.

NUTTY GREEN SALAD

    1 head crunchy romaine lettuce
    1 red pepper, sliced long and thin
    1–2 green onion stalks, diced
    1 cucumber, partially peeled and sliced into rounds
    1 head broccoli
    ½ cup sunflower seeds, soaked 3 hours and drained
    ½ cup raw almonds, soaked 3 hours and drained
    ½ cup raw sesame seed, ground to a meal

Tear lettuce into bite-sized pieces into a large bowl. Add red pepper, green onion stalks, and cucumber. Prepare broccoli as described in *Annie's Favorite Salad* (see recipe, p. 80) and add to bowl. Put soaked sunflower seed and almonds into blender and pulse blend a moment, or simply chop the almonds with a knife so that they're still chunky, and add to salad. Top with ground sesame seed, and serve tossed with *Whipped Walnut Dressing* (see recipe, p. 123).

CABBAGE SALAD

    1 small white cabbage
    1 carrot, finely grated
    1 handful clover sprouts

Fill sink with ice water and soak cabbage for a moment to crisp it up. Drain and shred it. Place in a bowl and toss with finely grated carrot. Put handful or two into individual bowls and top with favorite dressing. Add sprouts.

    Serves 2.

COLESLAW

1 medium head white cabbage, or half red and half white cabbage,
   shredded
¼ cup onion, minced
2 inches fresh ginger root, grated
¼ cup olive oil
2 tablespoon raw apple cider vinegar
1–3 garlic cloves, peeled and minced
½ cup fresh parsley, chopped finely
½ cup fresh dill, chopped finely
¼ cup prepared jar of mustard
2 tablespoons Shoyu soy sauce
1 tablespoon nutritional yeast
Celtic sea salt and freshly ground pepper, to taste
¼ cup capers (optional)

Soak cabbage in ice water until crisp. Prepare the dressing by combining all remaining ingredients in a large bowl. Mix well with a wooden spoon. Shred cabbage and toss into the dressing mixture. Toss everything well. Cover and let chill for 2 hours before serving. Leftovers keep well for a several days when covered in the refrigerator.

Makes about 7 servings.

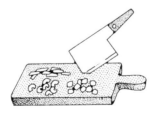

NUTTY LENTIL SALAD

¼ cup raw almond butter

4 tablespoons olive oil

½ cup charged water

5 cups lentil sprouts

3 tablespoons Bragg Liquid Aminos

2 cups celery, minced

1 tablespoon raw sesame tahini

1 red pepper

2 teaspoons nutritional yeast

2 green onions with tops, minced

2 teaspoons kelp

Soak lentils overnight and sprout for 2 days, rinsing them 2–3 times a day. You'll need about 3 cups of dry lentil for the required 5 cups of sprouts. Any extra lentils can be tossed into salads or made into pâté. Blend almond butter, olive oil, and charged water in blender to a smooth consistency. Put lentil sprouts through food processor. Place sprouts in a large bowl and add all other ingredients. Add the almond butter mixture and stir in well. Chill for several hours in refrigerator before serving. Serve as a salad or sandwich spread, or stuffed in avocado halves drizzled with a favorite dressing.

Makes 6–7 servings.

DILL SAUERKRAUT

2 heads cabbage, green, red, or combination of both
½ cup kelp powder
½ cup dry dill, or full bunch fresh dill, chopped
2 cups apple juice

Set aside 6–8 outer leaves of cabbage. Shred the rest of the cabbage and fill a 3-gallon pail, or kraut crock pot, to 3 inches with shreds. Sprinkle a heaping tablespoon each of kelp and dill over cabbage shreds. Repeat process until pail is filled. Pour apple juice over all, and cover with 6–8 outer leaves of cabbage.

Place a dish over the leaves and place a weight on top of that. Cover the top with a cloth. Leave at moderate room temperature for 7 days. Remove plate and discard outer leaves completely by skimming from side of container before removing sauerkraut. Store in jars in the refrigerator. Will stay good for one month.

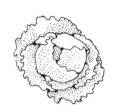

Secret Teaching: Sauerkraut contains a bountiful harvest of pre-digested proteins and sugars abundant with enzymes to help you digest your food. Cabbage has vitamin U, good for healing the digestive tract. Restore pH and friendly intestinal flora with this super nutritious food! It is a wonderful food for people healing from alcoholism and other gastrointestinal ailments. Sauerkraut is one of the most important foods of our time. We have almost no friendly fermented food in our diet today and a lack of friendly intestinal flora is at the roots of all disease. It's cheap, super easy to make and contains hundreds of millions more healthy bacteria than a store bought liquid acidophilus product.

TABOULI

2 cups quinoa sprouts, soaked 8 hours, sprouted 1–2 days, until soft
2 large fresh tomatoes, diced
1 cup parsley, chopped
1 green pepper, diced
2 green onions, diced
1 large cucumber, diced
½ cup cold-pressed oil (sesame or olive)
½ cup lemon juice
kelp powder and soy sauce, to taste

Soak 2 cups of quinoa and allow to sprout 1 full day. Dice tomatoes, parsley, green pepper, green onions, and cucumbers. Combine vegetables with sprouts. Mix oil and lemon juice together, and sprinkle with kelp powder and soy sauce to taste for dressing. Toss dressing into the other ingredients and chill for 2 hours. Keeps well in the refrigerator for 2 days.

Serves 4.

Secret Teaching: Parsley is a rich source of chromium and Vitamin B12. It's rare to find chromium at such high levels as it is in parsley. Chromium is helpful in blood sugar metabolism. Parsley and oil help manage release of sugar by the liver, making this an important dish for all hypoglycemic and diabetic people. Most Americans can benefit from eating a little parsley each day.

SAVORY SEA VEGETABLE DELIGHT

2 cup dry dulse seaweed
¼ head red cabbage, shredded
8–10 fresh shiitake mushrooms
⅛ cup ginger root, grated
3 tablespoons ground raw sesame seed
3 tablespoons flax seed oil
3 tablespoons safflower oil
2 tablespoons raw sesame tahini
2 tablespoons Bragg Liquid Aminos
1 tablespoon lemon juice

Soak dulse in spring water until soft (about 5 minutes) then drain. Put all ingredients in a food processor and pulse 30 seconds until stiff with chunks. Serve in small bowls.

Serves 4.

SEAWEED SALAD

2 cups soaked seaweed (hijiki or arame)
¼ cup raw apple cider vinegar
½ cup cold-pressed sesame oil
Dash toasted sesame oil
4 tablespoons Shoyu soy sauce, to taste
½ cup raw sesame seed, ground to a meal, to garnish

Arrange seaweed attractively into individual bowls. Blend other ingredients and pour over the seaweed. For a nice variation, try adding 1 tablespoon maple syrup or honey. Top with ground sesame seed.

Serves 4.

Secret Teaching: Sea vegetables contain a rich cache of highly absorbable, densely concentrated, life-supporting colloidal minerals. Enzymes in the raw apple cider vinegar marinade help the upper stomach break down the plant fiber—helping to release its cache of minerals. Sea vegetables contain iodine, which accelerates thyroid function and sets the metabolic weight, a very important step in healing obesity.

SUCCULENT SESAME SEA SALAD

1 package (about 2 ounces) hijiki seaweed
½ package dulse
½ package pacific palm frond, or arame
2 tablespoons olive oil
2 tablespoons raw apple cider vinegar
Dash toasted sesame oil
1 tablespoon Shoyu soy sauce
Dash Dr. Bronner's Mineral Bouillon
4 tablespoons ground raw sesame seeds, for garnish

Soak hijiki for 45 minutes; softer sea vegetables for 10 minutes or until soft, then drain well. Combine remaining ingredients to make the dressing using a shaking jar and mixing well. Pour over salad and toss. Garnish with lightly ground sesame seed. Serve with a crunchy green salad.

Serves 4 or 5.

FRESH CUCUMBERS

1 cucumber
2 tablespoons Garlic-chili flax seed oil
2 tablespoons Bragg Liquid Aminos
Dulse flakes, nutritional yeast, and Spirulina flakes, to garnish

Take a fresh, organic cucumber and slice it on the diagonal. Arrange attractively on a plate, and drizzle with garlic chili flax seed oil, or another cold-pressed oil, and Bragg Liquid Aminos. Sprinkle with dulse flakes, nutritional yeast, and Spirulina flakes.

Optional: Top cucumber with diced red onion and/or sauerkraut (see *Dill Saurkraut,* p. 87).

A lovely and mouth-watering side dish, or a meal for one!

MEXICAN CUCUMBERS

2 large fresh cucumbers
Celtic sea salt
½ cup lemon juice, fresh-squeezed
Cayenne pepper (optional)

Peel and slice cucumber on the diagonal. Put into large bowl and toss well with salt and lemon juice. Dust with cayenne powder if you choose. Let sit to absorb flavor for 20 minutes or more in the refrigerator. Toss again and serve.

A side dish for 4–6.

Secret Teaching: Cucumbers have a natural cooling property, thus, the old saying "cool as a cucumber."

HIJIKI & RED PEPPER SALAD

3 tablespoons flax seed oil
3 tablespoons raw apple cider vinegar
2 tablespoons sesame oil
2 tablespoons honey
1 tablespoon unpasteurized miso
3 tablespoons Bragg Liquid Aminos
2 tablespoons tahini
1 garlic clove, crushed
2 tablespoons fresh ginger, grated
1 package hijiki (about 2 ounces), soaked 1 hour until soft, then
    drained
2 red peppers, deseeded and sliced thin in long strips
1 medium cucumber, peeled and diced
1 medium zucchini, shredded

Blend oils, vinegar, honey, miso, Bragg Liquid Aminos, tahini, garlic, and ginger in a blender to make dressing. Toss dressing over remaining ingredients in a large bowl.

Serves 3–4.

WINTER'S MASH

¼ medium cauliflower
¼ small cabbage
1 small bok choy
1 cup mung bean sprouts
1 handful fresh basil

3 tablespoons ground raw sesame seed

3 tablespoons Shoyu soy sauce

1 tablespoons flax seed oil

3 tablespoons safflower oil

1 tablespoon raw clover honey

¾ cup peanuts, sprouted

½ cup charged water

1 ½ tablespoons raw apple cider vinegar

Wash and cut vegetables into small pieces. Blend all ingredients in a food processor or blender until mixture is stiff with chunks. Serve in small bowls.

Serves 4.

PEANUT GARLIC SHREDDED SALAD

2 garlic cloves, peeled and pressed

¼ cup cold-pressed olive oil

Freshly ground black pepper, to taste

⅔ cup sprouted organic peanuts

1 cup zucchini, peeled and shredded

2 small yams, peeled and shredded

Blend garlic, oil, and pepper in blender. Let stand covered all day at room temperature in a dark place. Shred yams and zucchini. Toss into the garlic mixture and combine. Chop the peanut sprouts lightly and sprinkle over top.

A side dish for 4 or 5.

WALNUT ZUCCHINI GREENS

1 head broccoli
½ head romaine, or red leaf lettuce
2 small zucchini, shredded
½ cup walnuts
3 tablespoons raw nutbutter (almond, hemp, or other)
2 tablespoons unpasteurized goat cheese, or seed cheese
3 tablespoons charged water
1 tablespoon kelp seasoning
1 tablespoon dill weed (dried dill)
1 tablespoon raw apple cider vinegar
½ cup orange juice
Celtic sea salt and fresh pepper, to taste

Lightly blanch broccoli by running hot tap water over head until it turns a bright green. Cut off flowerets and reserve stems for use in another dish. Arrange lettuce on a platter with broccoli flowerets. To make the sauce, shred the zucchini, then combine with remaining ingredients and blend in the food processor using the "S" blade. Drizzle sauce over the broccoli and lettuce. Salt and pepper to taste.

An elegant side dish for 4.

SWEET TOMATO SLICES

1 tablespoon raw apple cider vinegar
1 tablespoon olive or flax seed oil
3 figs, soaked in ½ cup water for 10 minutes
2 medium ripe red tomato, sliced thin
Ground pepper, to taste

Blend vinegar, oil, and figs with soak water in a blender and drizzle over tomato slices. Grind fresh pepper over the plate. Serve as a colorful and tasty side dish. A great recipe to jazz up hothouse tomatoes.

TOMATO & RED ONION SALAD

4 large sun-ripened organic tomatoes, sliced
½ red onion, sliced into thin rings
½ cup cold-pressed olive oil
¼ cup raw apple cider vinegar
½ cup mixture of thyme, rosemary, oregano, and/or basil
1 garlic clove
2 tablespoons unpasteurized blue cheese (optional)
Ground pepper, to taste
Basil leave, to garnish

Arrange tomato slices and big rings of red onion attractively on plate. Blend remaining ingredients in blender to make sauce and drizzle over tomatoes. Grind fresh pepper over the plate. Garnish with basil leaves.

Platter serves 6–8 side dishes.

AVOCADO SOAKED-SEED SALAD

2 cups lentil sprouts, sprouted 2 days
½ cup pine nuts
4 sun dried tomatoes, soaked until soft in 2 cups water
2 cups sunflower seeds, soaked a few hours and rinsed
2 avocados, cubed
1 large cucumber, peeled and diced
1 small red onion, minced
4 tablespoons olive oil
½ cup fresh basil
3 tablespoons raisins
1 tablespoon poppy seed
2 tablespoons raw apple cider vinegar
Soak water from sun-dried tomato
Freshly ground black pepper, to taste

Grind lentil sprouts and pine nuts lightly in food processor. Slice the soaked sun-dried tomatoes into thin lengths, reserving the soak water for the sauce. Place lentil sprouts, pine nuts, sun-dried tomatoes, sunflower seeds, avocados, and cucumber in a large bowl and toss to combine. Prepare the sauce by blending the remaining ingredients in a blender. Blend sauce in blender. Drizzle over salad mixings and toss lightly. Let stand at room temperature for 15 minutes to increase flavor.

Serves 4–6.

SUPER SANDWICHES

2 slices sprouted grain bread, toasted
½ avocado, mashed
Organic raw milk goat cheese (optional)
1 zucchini, finely shredded
Clover sprouts
Cayenne pepper, garlic powder, or kelp seasoning, to season
Dash Bragg Liquid Aminos, or Shoyu soy sauce, to taste
Drizzle garlic-chili flax seed oil or olive oil, to finish

An excellent transitional meal to vegetarianism, Super Sandwiches can replace hamburgers as America's favorite! Take 2 pieces of toast and spread mashed avocado onto one half and thin slices or shredded cheese on the other (if desired). Add a handful of shredded zucchini and a handful of sprouts over the cheese. Add seasonings, Bragg Liquid Aminos or Shoyu soy sauce, and oil of choice. Sit in a quiet place and enjoy!

Variations

- Red pepper slivers
- Sauerkraut
- Cucumber slices
- Mustard
- Tomato slices
- Marinated mushroom
- Red onion rings
- Seed cheese

NOTE: As you make the transition toward LifeFood, first choose raw milk cow or goat cheese. Goat milk is more like mother's milk than cow milk is. Vegan choices include: sesame tahini, or Hempini (hemp seed tahini), a nut or seed pâté like Teriyaki Pâté *(see recipe, p. 110).*

As you transition away from flour products, replace bread made from sprouted grain flour to Essene breads that are made directly from sprouted grains. Manna is one brand found in the freezer or refrigerated section of your health food store. Better yet, make your own Essene bread, or simply roll everything up in romaine lettuce or Sushi Nori Rolls *(see recipe, p. 98).*

ANGEL'S FOOD CASSEROLE

Variation of Super Sandwiches

Buy a loaf of Essene bread (Manna brand) from the refrigerated section of your health food store (or make your own, see recipe in Chapter 5: *Nut & Seed Specials).* Slice bread in half lengthwise and open it so the inside is facing up. Layer on your ingredients as in the Super Sandwich. This is a nice presentation when you have guests and want to have an already-assembled dish for the table.

SUSHI NORI ROLLS

   1 Nori seaweed sushi sheet, un-toasted
   ⅛ cup seed or nut pâté, like *Vegetable Pâté* (see recipe, p. 109)
   2 or 3 avocado spears
   10–12 long clover sprouts
   2–3 cucumber spears, very slender and long like chopsticks
   1–2 zucchini, shredded or slender spears
   Kelp powder or sesame seed, to season

Smear any pâté or seed cheese onto a quarter of an open nori sheet, lengthwise. Layer the vegetables over the pâté in a lengthwise strip in the center of the pâté. Sprinkle with kelp powder or sesame seed, or drizzle with any dressing. Roll each sheet sushi-style, by hand or with a sushi mat, sealing the end with a little water. Cut each roll into 6–8 pieces.

Arrange sliced rolls on a tray with a little pile of pickled ginger and wasabi (a Japanese horseradish made by adding a bit of water to a powder you can find at your health food store near the nori). Use a small bowl for Shoyu soy sauce. For a treat add a little ginger juice to your Shoyu. Be creative and invent your own rolls.

Variations for Nori Rolls

- Marinated burdock, shitake, or portobello mushroom
- Long slivers of green or red pepper
- Pickled ginger
- Umiboshi plum paste
- Seed cheese

SPICY GINGER TOFU

1½ cakes (about 8 ounces) unpasteurized firm tofu
2 tablespoons apple cider vinegar
3 tablespoons safflower oil
1 tablespoon honey or maple syrup
1 ½-inch piece ginger, finely grated
1 teaspoon liquid lecithin
1 tablespoon unpasteurized miso
3 tablespoons Bragg Liquid Aminos
Dash cayenne and garlic powder
Oregano, to garnish

Cut tofu into "chopsticks" (¼-inch squares that are 1½ inches in length) and dry wrapped in a towel for an hour. Mix all other ingredients in a shaking jar and shake well. Place tofu in a long dish and pour sauce over. Garnish with dash of cayenne pepper, garlic powder, and oregano.

A side dish for 4.

Secret Teaching: Ginger increases blood flow to the extremities keeping the body warm in chilly climates. Ginger is very soothing to the stomach.

SUN-RICH YAMS—India style!

⅛ cup sesame, olive, or safflower oil
⅛ tablespoon cayenne pepper powder, to taste
2 medium organic yams, peeled and cut to match sticks

Mix the oil and cayenne powder well. Place yams in a bowl and toss well with the cayenne and oil. Place in the sun for a few hours or all day with a screen over the top. Serve as a side dish. The yams become super-charged from the sun.

SPICY GINGER SHIITAKE

1 cup sprouted grain: millet or wheat

½ cup sesame seed, ground to a moist meal

1 4-inch piece organic ginger root

¼ cup flax seed oil

1 tablespoon raw honey

2 small hot green chili peppers, deseeded and finely chopped

2 tablespoons raw apple cider vinegar

4 tablespoons Bragg Liquid Aminos

10–12 fresh shiitake mushrooms

2 broccoli stalks

1 red bell pepper, seeded & sliced into long thin strips

Tomatoes and parsley, chopped, to garnish

Lightly cut the grain in food processor with the "S" blade. Grind the sesame seed in grinder. Either grate the ginger very finely or juice it. Make a sauce by blending the ginger, oil, honey, hot peppers, vinegar, and Bragg Liquid Aminos. Slice shiitake mushrooms into chopstick width strips and marinade in sauce for ½ hour.

Shave flowerets of broccoli (reserve the stem for another dish) and mix with the grain and bell peppers. Arrange on a platter, drizzle with dressing, and sprinkle ground sesame seed liberally. Garnish with tomatoes and parsley. A very rich dish. Best served with a plain crunchy green salad.

Serves 4–6.

BBQ CAULIFLOWER

1 large head cauliflower, or 2 small

2 cups bean sprouts

1 cup sunflower seeds, soaked a few hours, then rinsed

10 sun-dried tomato slices, soaked in 1 ½ cups charged water, until soft

2 ripe tomatoes

4 tablespoons olive oil

4 tablespoons vinegar

2 tablespoons honey, or maple syrup, or 10 raisins

1 teaspoon chili powder

Cayenne powder, to taste

1 teaspoon ginger powder

1 cup *Rejuvelac* (see recipe, p. 190), or apple juice

Bragg Liquid Aminos, to taste

Garlic powder, to taste

Wash and cut cauliflower into bite-sized pieces and place in bowl with bean sprouts and soaked sunflower seeds. Soak sun-dried tomatoes in charged water until soft (usually a few hours). Blend soaked sun-dried tomatoes with soak water and the remaining ingredients in blender. Pour sauce over cauliflower mixture. Toss well. Marinade 2 hours or more in the refrigerator. Toss again and serve.

A side dish for 4–6.

Secret Teaching: Cruciferous vegetables like cauliflower have goitrogens (thyroid regulating agents) that help balance the endocrine system.

SWEET & SOUR ASPARAGUS

2 pounds young tender asparagus

⅔ cup raw apple cider vinegar

½ cup charged water

¼ cup cold-pressed safflower oil, or other oil

3 tablespoons Bragg Liquid Aminos

⅔ cup raw honey

⅔ tablespoon cinnamon

1 teaspoon clove, ground

1 teaspoon celery seed, ground

Peel the asparagus stalks if desired and place in a shallow glass dish. Otherwise rinse and place as are in dish. Mix all other ingredients in a blender, or a shaking jar, and pour over asparagus. Cover and chill for 24 hours. Drain before serving. Reserve the marinade and use for another vegetable, like zucchini or broccoli. It keeps well for a few days.

A side dish for 4.

TERIYAKI VEGETABLES — Spicy!

½ cup Bragg Liquid Aminos
½ teaspoon crushed red pepper
cayenne powder, to taste
2 tablespoons raw honey
Sprinkle of garlic powder and ginger powder

Vegetables of choice

- cauliflower
- broccoli
- bean sprouts
- sweat peas
- red and green peppers
- mushrooms

Mix sauce well. Pour over your favorite vegetable combo, choosing from those listed or using your own favorites. Use about 2 lbs. of vegetables, sliced and cut into bite-sized shapes. Make sure that tough vegetables like cauliflower and broccoli are small enough to become tender and flavorful in the marinade. Allow to marinate 2 hours at room temperature, stirring occasionally. Keeps well in the fridge for a day or two.

DLT: DULSE, LETTUCE, & TOMATO SANDWICH

2 slices sprouted grain bread, toasted
2 tablespoons coconut oil
2–4 thin tissue-like pieces of dulse
½ avocado
1 small handful lettuce, shredded
½ tomato, sliced
Cucumber, thinly sliced
1 zucchini, finely shredded

Clover sprouts

Cayenne pepper, garlic powder, kelp seasoning, or mustard, to
    season

Dash Bragg Liquid Aminos, or Shoyu soy sauce, to taste

Drizzle garlic-chili flax seed oil or olive oil, to finish

Take 2 slices of Manna brand bread, or other sprouted grain bread. Heat a skillet with a little coconut oil. When hot, quickly pan-fry some dulse on both sides, until crispy. Each side only takes a few seconds when the oil is hot; when the dulse changes to a light brown color immediately remove from pan and let it drain onto paper towels.

Prepare sandwich as in *Super Sandwiches* (see recipe, p. 97) with mashed avocado, lettuce, tomato slices, thinly sliced cucumber, shredded zucchini, and sprouts. Layer on the dulse. Dulse tastes very woodsy and is fragrant, rich, and crispy. This is a very tasty sandwich. Season with Bragg Liquid Aminos or soy sauce, cayenne pepper, garlic powder, kelp powder, or mustard, and drizzle with oil to finish.

> *NOTE: This is a special treat and should be prepared occasionally, especially*
> *when luring unsuspecting carnivores into enjoying a vegetarian meal.*
> *A great treat for kids, and those new to this way of eating.*

ZUCCHINI PASTA

> 1 small to medium zucchini per person
> (or half zucchini and half root vegetable, like turnip or rutabaga)

Run zucchini (or other vegetable) through shredder on food processor for long thin "spaghetti" or simply shred by hand. Rinse and allow to drain in colander for a few minutes. One handful of shredded zucchini per person is a good serving amount. Top with *Italian Tomato Sauce* or *Pesto Sauce* (see recipes, below).

ITALIAN TOMATO SAUCE

> 6 large fresh vine-ripened organic tomatoes, ⅓ chopped into chunks,
>   ⅔ pureed in blender
> 2 garlic cloves, peeled and crushed
> ½ cup fresh basil and oregano, mixed
> 2 tablespoons dried Italian herb mixture
> Fresh black pepper, to taste
> ½ onion, minced
> ¾ cup pecans, ground to a moist meal
> 2 cups *Rejuvelac* (see recipe, p. 190), or charged water
> ½ cup cold-pressed olive oil
> ¼ cup raw apple cider vinegar, or organic wine
> 2 tablespoons raw honey
> Dash of cinnamon
> 7 large button mushrooms, diced

Blend all ingredients except mushrooms in blender. Toss with mushrooms and serve, or warm if you like. Serve over *Zucchini Pasta* (see recipe, above).

> A main dish for 4–6.

PESTO SAUCE

1 large bunch of fresh basil

1 cup pine nuts or walnuts, or combine both

2 cloves fresh garlic, peeled and crushed

1 cup olive oil

Fresh black pepper, to taste

2 tablespoons brewers yeast, or 3 tablespoons raw milk Parmesan
cheese

Chop the basil together with the nuts for a few seconds in a food processor. Add all ingredients and pulse into a thick and chunky paste. Serve tossed with *Zucchini Pasta* (see recipe, p. 106).

Secret Teaching: Basil has bactericidal properties (hygienic to the body). It is a vermafuge (helps clear parasites), and it helps sedate muscles. It is very helpful for the kidneys and liver. Green is clean! Apart from the chlorophyll basil also contains Vitamins A and C.

OIL & GARLIC "PASTA"

½ cup olive oil
3 fresh garlic cloves, crushed
Fresh ground black pepper, to taste
5 sun-dried tomatoes, soak in water until soft, about an hour, drain
1 medium zucchini, shredded
1 medium carrot, shredded
⅛ cup unpasteurized Parmesan cheese (optional)
1 fresh tomato, chopped
Pinch of Celtic sea salt, to taste
Pinch of fresh ground pepper, to taste

Early in the day, blend the oil, garlic, and pepper well in a blender. Cut sun-dried tomatoes into thin long slices. Allow mixture to absorb flavor in a sealed glass jar with sun-dried tomatoes in a dark place at room temperature for several hours. Toss the sun-dried tomatoes with the shredded zucchini and carrots and oil mixture. Arrange in a bowl. Toss chopped tomatoes over the top and grind fresh black pepper and a pinch of Celtic sea salt to finish. A main dish for 4. Serve with a crunchy green salad.

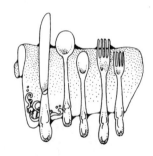

VEGETABLE PÂTÉ

    1 cup pumpkin seed, soaked 1 hour, drained and rinsed
    1 cup sunflower seeds, soaked 1 hour, drained and rinsed
    1 cup raw almonds, soaked 1 hour, drained and rinsed
    1 cup shredded zucchini
    ¼ cup white onion, chopped
    1 red pepper, deseeded and diced
    3 tablespoons lemon juice
    2 fresh garlic cloves, crushed
    3 tablespoons kelp, or dulse powder
    2 tablespoons nutritional yeast
    2 tablespoons ginger root, grated or juiced
    ⅔ cup *Rejuvelac* (see recipe, p. 190), nut milk, or water
    ¼ cup Shoyu soy sauce

Soak pumpkin, sunflower, and almonds for one hour in charged water. Drain and rinse them well with fresh water. Always discard soak water from seeds and nuts (see *Sprouting,* p. 57).

Grind soaked nuts and seeds with the other ingredients in a food processor with the "S" blade. Blend to a smooth paste. This is great Nori Roll filler, as a side to your favorite salad, or as a stuffing for half an avocado. Keeps well sealed in the refrigerator for several days.

TERIYAKI PÂTÉ

1 cup sunflower seeds, soaked 1 hour, drained and rinsed
1 cup almonds, soaked 1 hour, drained and rinsed
1 cup pumpkin seeds, soaked 1 hour, drained and rinsed
½ cup raisins, soaked 1 hour, drained and rinsed, soak water reserved
½ cup Bragg Liquid Aminos
1 red pepper, seeded and chopped
¼ onion, chopped
2 garlic cloves, peeled and crushed
1 piece 2-inch ginger root, peeled and crushed or juiced
Charged water, to finish

Soak pumpkin, sunflower, and almonds for one hour in charged water. Drain and rinse them well with fresh water. Always discard soak water from seeds and nuts (see *Sprouting,* p. 57). Separately soak raisins with ½ cup charged water for 1 hour. Keep the soak water of the raisins.

Blend rinsed nuts and seeds with raisins, their soak water, and Bragg Liquid Aminos into a paste using the "S" blade on the food processor. Take your time as the nuts and seeds should be added slowly to be easy on your machine. While machine is running, add red pepper, onion, garlic, and ginger. Add charged water to mixture for blending ease if needed. More water makes a smoother paste; less water makes a chunkier pâté.

This pâté is very special and a favorite. Serve as a side dish with sliced tomatoes. Spread onto nori seaweed paper to make dehydrated crackers (see Chapter 5, *Nut & Seed Specials*), or roll into *Nori Rolls* with other vegetables. Great as is on lettuce. Keeps well sealed in the refrigerator for several days.

HOT CURRY PÂTÉ

3 cups soaked nuts or seeds (sunflower, almond, sesame, pumpkin,
    walnut, or combination)

2 cups zucchini, shredded

1 small sweet onion

½ cup lemon juice, fresh-squeezed

2–3 fresh garlic cloves, crushed

½ habanero hot pepper, or other

2 heaping tablespoons mild or hot curry powder

3 tablespoons coconut butter, or olive oil

1 cup fresh parsley, rosemary, thyme, sorrel, cilantro, basil (any
    combination), loosely packed

3 tablespoons miso dissolved into 1 cup warm, charged water

Soak seed/nuts for a few hours, drain and rinse them well, discarding
soak water. Grind all ingredients together well in a food processor until
smooth. A filling winter dish with a salad, a great filling for dehydrated
treats like *Liscious Snacks* (see recipe, p. 139), and it also goes well in
the *Sushi Nori Rolls* (see recipe, p. 98). Keeps well sealed in the refrigerator for several days.

Makes about 6 cups.

GUACAMOLE

> 3 ripe avocados, diced (not mashed!)
> 2 medium tomatoes, cubed
> ½ red onion, diced
> 2–3 fresh cilantro sprigs, chopped
> Generous squirt Bragg Liquid Aminos
> 2 fresh garlic cloves, peeled and crushed
> 1 lemon or 1 orange, juiced (about ¼ cup)
> ⅛ tablespoon cayenne, or 1 jalapeño pepper, diced (optional)

Diced avocado is much more flavorful than mashed. Prepare ingredients, combine in large bowl, and toss well. This is easy party food and great when served with cucumber slices or crisp lettuce leaves for scooping. If you have any leftovers, store in the refrigerator with the avocado pits back in the guacamole. The enzyme inhibitors covering the pit will keep the it fresher.

STUFFED AVOCADO

Slice avocados in half, remove pits, and carefully peel off skin. Slice a base off the back of the avocado so it will sit on its back.

The possible fillings are endless. Here are some suggestions:

- Spicy Ginger Shiitake
- Teriyaki Pâté, or any pâté
- Sauerkraut
- Any dressing

Garnish with red pepper, ground sesame seed, oil, soy sauce, spirulina, and cayenne. A filling meal for 2 when served with a crunchy green salad.

AZTEC QUICHE

   4 cups sprouted quinoa

   1 cup sunflower seeds, soaked 1 hour, drained and rinsed

   4 tablespoons cold-pressed sesame oil, or other oil

   3 tablespoons maple syrup, raw honey, or raisins

   3 tablespoons raisins, soaked in ¼ cup charge water for 20 minutes,
       reserve water

   2 tablespoons unpasteurized miso

   6 tablespoons spirulina (lecithin flakes is best)

   2 cups ground seed, sesame or pumpkin

   Tabasco hot sauce, or cayenne powder

   3 cups zucchini, shredded

   2 tomatoes, diced

   3 tablespoons cold-pressed oil (for sauce)

   3 tablespoons vinegar

   2 tablespoons miso

   ½ cucumber, peeled and diced

   1 garlic clove, diced

   2 tablespoons slippery elm powder*

   Dulse flakes, to season

Run sprouted quinoa and sunflower seed through food processor until smooth. Grease a pie plate or small casserole dish with toasted sesame seed oil (or other oil). Firmly press grain and seed mixture evenly to form your crust. Smear honey or maple syrup over the crust very thinly, or if using raisins, blend raisins in with soak water. Next, smear a thin layer of miso.

LifeFood Recipe Book

Sprinkle generous amounts of the spirulina flakes over the miso layer. The flakes really make the quiche special. Grind seeds to a moist meal, and shake half of it over quiche. Tabasco or cayenne powder goes on next. Layer on tomatoes and zucchini and drizzle oil over them. Add another layer of spirulina flakes and then the rest of the ground seed.

To make the sauce, blend up the oil and vinegar with the miso (2 tablespoons), cucumber, garlic clove, and slippery elm powder. As an alternative, serve with *Green Goddess Dressing* (see recipe, p. 122), adding 2 tablespoons slippery elm powder. Drizzle sauce over the quiche. Cool for 2 hours in the refrigerator to set. Crumble the dulse flakes over the top.

> * Buy slippery elm powder in loose-tea form in the herb section of your health food store.

CHAPTER 3

DRESSING, SAUCE, & MARINADE

LifeFood dishes look better and taste better than cooked food. Flavorful sauces can transform food into a delightful experience. Invent your own sauces, using these recipes to stimulate your creativity. These recipes will keep fresh for several days, sealed in the refrigerator. Marinade sauce can be used twice, if used again within a day or two, by simply adding more vegetables and letting them soak for a few hours.

The resourceful chef will use any remaining marinade sauce as a start for a soup or dressing. Create a new dressing by extending remaining marinade sauce with: oil and vinegar; a nut/seed milk; or simply coconut water with lemon or lime juice. Add your favorite seasonings, herbs, and vegetables. Blend well. The possibilities are endless!

DILL VINAIGRETTE

¼ –⅓ cup cold-pressed olive oil

½ cup raw apple cider vinegar

3 tablespoons Shoyu soy sauce

1 tablespoon raw sesame tahini

1 tablespoon raw honey

½ tablespoon miso

1 fresh garlic clove, peeled and crushed

3 bushy fresh dill sprigs, chopped, or 3 tablespoons dried dill

3 tablespoons Bragg Liquid Aminos

Blend all ingredients well in a blender or shaking jar.

Makes about 1 cup.

TAHINI TAMARI DRESSING

½ cup olive oil, or other oil

1 lemon, juiced

¼ cup raw sesame seed, un-hulled

⅓ cup Shoyu soy sauce

¼ cup charged water, or *Rejuvelac* (see recipe, p. 190)

2 teaspoons kelp, or dulse powder

1 garlic clove, peeled and crushed

1 tablespoon ginger powder, or fresh grated ginger

Blend all ingredients well in blender or shaking jar.

Makes about 1½ cups.

Secret Teaching: Un-hulled sesame seeds contain a significant source of organic calcium, important for good liver function. Organic calcium helps balance a sugar from a starch. This is important to remember when using hybrid vegetables, such as carrots and beets. Adding un-hulled sesame seed, ground to a moist meal, more easily assimilates starchy vegetables and high glycemic foods.

DILL DIJON DRESSING

3–4 tablespoons Dijon mustard (from a store-bought jar rather than
    mustard powder)
3 tablespoons Shoyu soy sauce
¼ cup raw apple cider vinegar
1 tablespoon raw sesame tahini
¼ cup olive oil
½ lemon, juiced
3 bushy fresh dill sprigs, chopped, or 3 tablespoons dried dill
1 tablespoon honey, or raisins
¼ cup *Rejuvelac* (see recipe, p. 190), or charged water

Blend all ingredients well in blender.

    Makes about 1 cup.

FRESH HERB DRESSING

¼ cup olive oil, or other oil

¼ cup raw apple cider vinegar

¼ cup apple cider, or juice

2 tablespoons raw sesame tahini

2 tablespoons honey, or 10 raisins

3 tablespoons flax seed oil

1 tablespoon grated ginger root

½ cup fresh dill, rosemary, and thyme (combined)

Blend all ingredients well in blender.

Makes about 1 cup.

BUTTERNUT TAHINI DRESSING

1 cup butternut squash, peeled, seeded, and shredded

1 tablespoon raw sesame tahini

3 tablespoons cold-pressed olive oil, or liquid coconut butter

3 tablespoons raw apple cider vinegar

1 tablespoon nutritional yeast

2 tablespoons tamari, to taste

½ tablespoon turmeric powder (optional)

Dash of toasted sesame oil

Pinch Celtic sea salt

Charged water, nut milk, or Rejuvelac to blend, about ⅓ cup.

Blend all ingredients in blender until smooth.

Makes about 1½ cups.

ZESTY HERB DRESSING

2⅓ cups cold-pressed olive oil, or other oil
⅔ cup unpasteurized apple cider vinegar
2 basil sprigs, or parsley
2 lemons, juiced
1 tablespoon unpasteurized miso
½ jalapeño
1 teaspoon thyme
1 celery stalk
1 teaspoon kelp
1 bell pepper, finely chopped
2 tablespoons Shoyu soy sauce
Pinch Celtic sea salt

Blend all ingredients in blender. Keeps in refrigerator 2 or 3 days.

Makes about 3 cups.

POMEGRANATE VINAIGRETTE

½ cup pomegranate juice
¼ cup raw apple cider vinegar
⅓ cup olive oil
2 tablespoons raw sesame tahini
Dash garlic powder
Dash onion powder

Seed the pomegranate and juice the seeds. Add juice and all other ingredients to blender and blend well. Delicious over cabbage salad.

Serves 2 or 3.

LEMON GINGER DRESSING

1½–2 lemons, peeled and juiced
1 piece 2-inch ginger root, grated
⅛ cup olive oil
3 tablespoons Shoyu soy sauce
1 fresh garlic clove, peeled and crushed
3 tablespoons unpasteurized miso
3 tablespoons raw honey

Mix all ingredients well in shaking jar. Toss with a yummy green salad.

Makes about ½ cup.

Secret Teaching: The lemon and ginger in this recipe combine to improve lymph and blood circulation. A sun-ripened lemon has over 200 enzymes making lemons one of the most restorative foods for the liver. It has a special type of calcium that grows toward the sunlight (anionic). This is important in restoring the liver, as the livers secretions are anionic.

GARLIC LEMON DRESSING

2 whole lemons, juiced
¼ cup flax seed oil
¼ cup olive oil
3/4 cup fresh apple juice
2 tablespoons raw apple cider vinegar
3–4 garlic cloves
2½ tablespoons mellow white miso
¼ cup raw honey
½ teaspoon Celtic sea salt
¼ teaspoon cayenne powder
¼ cup Bragg Liquid Aminos
3 tablespoons Dr. Bronner's Mineral Bouillon (optional)
1 tablespoon ginger root, grated

Blend all ingredients well in blender.

Makes about 2 cups.

CREAMY ALMOND DRESSING

1 cup almonds, soaked 1 hour, drained and rinsed well
½ bell pepper, yellow or red
1 lemon, juiced
1 fresh garlic clove, peeled and crushed
1 piece 1½-inch ginger root, shredded
3 tablespoons rosemary needles or other fresh herb like parsley
1 handful beets, shredded
½ cup *Rejuvelac* (see recipe, p. 190), or charged water
1 tablespoon unpasteurized miso
½ tablespoon Celtic sea salt
2 tablespoons raw honey
1 tablespoon raw sesame tahini

Blend all ingredients well in blender. It's colorful and delicious.

Makes about 2 cups.

GREEN GODDESS DRESSING

1 ripe avocado, chopped
½ red pepper, deseeded and diced
1 garlic clove, peeled and crushed
1 lemon, juiced

¼ cup *Rejuvelac* (see recipe, p. 190), or charged water

1 small tomato, cubed

1 small cucumber, peeled and diced

⅛ cup Bragg Liquid Aminos

1 teaspoon unpasteurized miso

1 tablespoon soy lecithin

1 tablespoon raw honey

1 tablespoon raw sesame tahini

Pinch Celtic sea salt

Blend all ingredients well in a blender. Add additional *Rejuvelac* or charged water to thin.

Makes about 1½ cups.

WHIPPED WALNUT DRESSING

1 cup raw walnuts, soaked 10 minutes, then drained

1 medium red pepper, deseeded and chopped

¼ cup *Rejuvelac* (see recipe, p. 190), or charged water

3 tablespoons raw apple cider vinegar

3 tablespoons Bragg Liquid Aminos

2 tablespoons each: dried parsley, dill, oregano, and sage

3 tablespoons flax seed oil

3 tablespoons safflower oil

1 lemon, juiced

1 teaspoon powdered garlic

1 teaspoon powdered ginger

1 teaspoon unpasteurized miso

Blend all ingredients well in blender until creamy and smooth.

Makes about 2 cups.

HOT SAUCE

2 cups tomatoes, chopped
½ red onion, minced
1 large garlic clove, crushed
½ cup green pepper, chopped
1 tablespoon apple cider vinegar
1 fresh green, yellow, or red hot pepper, deseeded and diced
1 tablespoon raw honey
Good pinch Celtic sea salt

Combine all ingredients and blend well.
Cover tightly to keep in refrigerator.

Makes about 3 cups.

GREEN MOLE

8 medium green tomatillos, peeled and chopped
1 bunch cilantro

Blend all ingredients well in blender. Serve with cucumber slices instead of chips. Great as a sauce or a dip.

Makes about 1½ cups.

WALNUT HONEY CHUTNEY

¼ cup charged water
¼ cup raw clover honey
1 teaspoon ground cinnamon
2 cups raw walnuts, chopped

Blend water with honey and cinnamon. Toss with walnuts. Serve as a condiment with dinner or dessert. Store in a tightly capped glass jar.

They're nice as is, or dehydrate them at 118°F for a few hours, or overnight. Serve warm over a green salad for a real treat.

Makes about 2½ cups.

MANGO CHUTNEY

1 ripe mango, pitted and chopped
2 cups tart plum, pitted and chopped
3 tablespoons raw honey
½ red onion, chopped
2 garlic cloves, crushed
⅛ teaspoon cayenne powder
3 tablespoons Dr. Bronner's Mineral Bouillon
2 tablespoons raw apple cider vinegar
Peel of ¼ lemon into thin match sticks, or zest curls
¼ cup ground coconut
2 tablespoons flax seed oil
½ lemon, juiced with pulp
½ teaspoon cinnamon

Mix all ingredients together and let the flavors marry for several days. Keeps in refrigerator for weeks.

Makes about 3½ cups.

HONEY MARMALADE

2 cups raw creamed honey
¾ cup orange and lemon peel, shredded or zest curls

Combine all ingredients well, adding a little citrus juice to blend well. Let flavor for a few days. Stir well before serving.

Makes 2¾ cups.

SPICY THAI PEANUT SAUCE

    1½ cup organic sprouted peanuts, or ½ cup raw peanut butter
    ¼ cup cold-pressed oil
    2 tablespoons raw apple cider vinegar
    1 teaspoon cayenne powder
    1 fresh garlic clove, crushed

Soak peanut sprouts overnight and sprout 5 days; Texas sprouting peanuts are best here (for ordering, see p. 54). Grind sprouted peanuts lightly in a food processor. Add remaining ingredients and grind well. Serve over long strips of zucchini, or on a crunchy green salad with cucumbers.

NOTE: Regular peanuts and peanut butter found in most stores contain mold. It is very important to use an excellent organic source.

MAYONNAISE

    ½ cup lemon juice, fresh-squeezed
    3 tablespoons raw sesame tahini
    ¼ cup cold-pressed oil
    1 teaspoon dulse or kelp, ground

Blend lemon juice and tahini at low speed and slowly add oil. Add more oil for a thinner mayonnaise or less oil for thicker mayonnaise. Store capped in refrigerator.

    Makes about 1 cup.

PISTACHIO MAYONNAISE

½ cup raw pistachio nuts, shelled
1 cup charged water or *Rejuvelac* (see recipe, p. 190)
1 teaspoon kelp powder
½ teaspoon paprika
1 cup walnut or pumpkin seed oil, or other oil
2 lemons, juiced

In a blender/food processor, blend the pistachios, charged water, kelp powder, and paprika lightly. Slowly adding in the lemon and oil while maintaining a slow speed until all ingredients are combined and mayonnaise obtains desired consistency. It should be very rich and creamy.

Makes 2½ cups.

CREAMY AVOCADO MAYONNAISE

1 cup pecans
2 avocados
3 tablespoons walnut oil (or other cold-pressed oil)
2 tablespoons raw honey
⅓ cup charged water, or *Rejuvelac* (see recipe, p. 190)

Grind pecans to a meal. Place oil and avocado in a blender and blend lightly. Slowly add in the nuts and the honey, blending until mayonnaise obtains smooth consistency.

Makes about 2 cups.

MARINADE for BURDOCK ROOT or SHIITAKE

2 tablespoons raw honey

4 tablespoons Shoyu soy sauce

½ cup *Rejuvelac* (see recipe, p. 190), or charged water

2 tablespoons Bragg Liquid Aminos

1 teaspoon sesame oil

Dash toasted sesame oil (optional)

2 tablespoons sesame seeds

Mix all ingredients together in a bowl large enough to accommodate burdock root or shiitake. Cut burdock into chopstick-width slices, 3 inches in length. If using shiitake, leave whole. Marinate 2 hours, tossing occasionally. Serve in sauce. Makes about 1 cup of sauce to marinade about 2 pounds of burdock or 15–20 shiitake mushrooms.

Secret Teaching: shiitake mushroom is a strengthening and restorative food that contains polysaccharides, which are very important in modulating good immune functioning. The active polysaccharides have anti-tumor, anti-viral, and immune cell activation properties and stimulate antibody, prostaglandin, and interferon synthesis and production. Shiitake contains eritadinon, a substance that lowers cholesterol.

Burdock root has Para-Amino Benzoic Acid (PABA), which is uncommon to most foods. Excellent for maintaining and reviving hair color, integrity of skin, and helpful in producing folic acid. PABA also aids in the metabolism of protein and blood formation.

HOT SESAME MARINADE

1 tablespoon fresh ginger, minced
2 large garlic cloves, crushed
¼ cup Shoyu soy sauce
4 tablespoons honey
½ lemon, juiced
2 tablespoons raw apple cider vinegar
1 tablespoon sesame oil
2 tablespoons sesame seeds
5 tablespoons *Hot Sauce* (see recipe, p. 124), or Tabasco sauce

Mix all ingredients together in a bowl large enough to accommodate 2–3 pounds of the prepared vegetables of your choice (zucchini, broccoli, shiitake mushrooms, bean sprouts, bok choy). Marinate 2 hours, drain, and serve.

ORANGE PECAN MARINADE

Grated rind of 1 orange (zest)
½ cup orange juice, fresh-squeezed
½ lemon, juiced
¼ cup olive oil
2 tablespoons honey
¼ cup pecans, chopped very fine
⅛ teaspoon ground clove
Pinch dry mustard

Mix all ingredients together in a large bowl. Toss with 2–3 pounds of your favorite vegetable, like zucchini slices, or a combination, such as broccoli and Chinese bean sprouts with thin slices of red pepper. Marinate 2 hours, drain, and serve.

PINEAPPLE TERIYAKI MARINADE

¾ cup Bragg Liquid Aminos
2 tablespoons flax seed oil
2 tablespoons raw honey
½ cup pineapple juice with pulp
3 large garlic cloves, peeled and pressed
Dash cayenne powder

Combine all ingredients in a large bowl. Toss with 2 or 3 pounds of your favorite fresh vegetables: yellow and green squash, shredded cabbage, cauliflower, blanched broccoli, soaked sunflower seeds, asparagus, etc. Marinate for 2 hours. Delicious when served over *Dinner Grains* (see recipe, p. 156).

SWEET KOREAN MARINADE

3 tablespoons Shoyu soy sauce
3 tablespoons raw apple cider vinegar
2 tablespoons raw honey
2 large garlic clove, peeled and pressed
2 tablespoons ginger root, pressed or grated
2 tablespoons sesame seeds
1 tablespoon cold-pressed sesame oil
Freshly ground black pepper

Mix all ingredients well in a large bowl. Add 2 pounds of your favorite prepared vegetables like: zucchini, shredded carrot, leeks, mushrooms, etc. Marinate 2 hours, drain, and serve.

SESAME SALT SEASONING

1 cup Celtic Sea salt
1 cup charged water
¼ cup sesame seeds

Dissolve 2 tablespoons of Celtic sea salt in 1 cup charged water in a bowl. Add sesame seeds and let soak in salt brine for 6 hours. Remove seeds with a strainer and discard brine. Put seeds into heated skillet until seeds are brown and just able to crumble between your fingers. Remove seeds from skillet and place the Celtic sea salt into the skillet until the salt becomes dryer. Note: you want the salt to remain damp! Just heat it until about half of the moisture is gone.

Add sesame seeds to the skillet with the salt and pan fry ingredients together until most of the salt's dampness is gone, then remove from heat immediately. Grind in a grinder. Store the salt in a sealed glass jar. This seasoning can be used to enhance the flavor of food, while helping you to digest the carbohydrates, proteins, and fats in your meal. Read more about the benefits of Celtic sea salt (p. 49).

CHAPTER 4

DEHYDRATED DISHES

Foods become more concentrated in their mineral and vitamin content when properly dehydrated under 118°F. Food can be stored at room temperature after dehydration and therefore its life can be significantly extended, and it is more transportable. Dehydrated dishes are denser and should be chewed thoroughly. They provide a heartier fare for those that work and play hard.

Dehydrate fruit and vegetables by slicing or blending them down in a blender. Then lay or pour onto dehydration sheets and dehydrate at 118°F until moisture is low. Dehydrating is an ancient method to preserve very ripe food that needs to be eaten now or dehydrated for storage and later consumption.

TAMARI ALMONDS

> 3 cups raw almonds
> ¼ cup Shoyu soy sauce, or Bragg Liquid Aminos
> Garlic powder, to taste
> Cayenne powder, to taste
> Dr. Bronner's Balanced Protein-Seasoning Powder (optional)

Soak almonds for 1 hour, then drain and rinse them well. Always discard soak water from nuts and seeds. Combine almonds, soy sauce or Bragg Liquid Aminos, and garlic and cayenne powder in a bowl and toss well. Allow flavors to meld for a few hours then toss again. Spread evenly on a teflex dehydrator sheet, or a shallow pan. If you choose to use Dr. Bronner's powder, shake over the almonds. This gives a nice woodsy taste.

Dehydrate at 118°F for several hours until dry, or sun bake them on a hot day for a few hours until dry. In the city, dry them indoors on a radiator, or in your pre-warmed oven on the lowest temperature for 7 minutes, stirring twice. When you remove them from the oven, stir them up and transfer them to your wooden cutting board to cool. Store them sealed; they needn't be refrigerated, though they stay fresher when they are. These are great for hiking and traveling—a protein-powered food.

> *Secret Teaching: The tamari and vegetable minerals from Dr. Bronner's powder increase digestive forces to better assimilate the dried nut. Always chew nuts (and everything else) to a liquid!*

TAMARI GARLIC SPROUTED PEANUTS

> 4 cups Texas sprouting peanuts, soaked 8 hours, sprouted 5 days
> ¼ cup Bragg Liquid Aminos
> Garlic powder to taste

Toss peanut sprouts in Bragg Liquid Aminos and let sit for a few hours. Toss again and transfer peanuts to a dehydrator tray with the teflex sheet. Spread them out evenly and shake garlic powder over them. Dehydrate them at 118°F for several hours until dried. Remove the teflex sheets and dry or one more hour on the dehydrator screens. These peanuts are very tasty! A good transition food for peanut butter junkies who want to leave it behind. (Peanuts are challenging to digest and peanut butter is famous for lining the intestinal tract.)

> NOTE: *Regular peanuts and peanut butter found in most stores contain mold. It is extremely important to use an excellent source like the Sprout House (see www.sprouthouse.com).*

SWEET TERIYAKI ALMONDS

    8 cups almonds
    2 cups Bragg Liquid Aminos, or Shoyu soy sauce
    ½ cup maple syrup, or raw honey
    1 garlic clove, peeled and pressed
    ½ jalapeño pepper

Soak almonds for 1 hour, then drain and rinse them well. Always discard soak water from nuts and seeds. Blend sauce in blender for 30 seconds. Put nuts into marinade bowl with sauce. Let sit for an hour, stirring occasionally. Place on teflex sheets and dehydrate at 118°F for 5 hours or more until tops of nuts are dry. Remove from teflex sheet and onto screened dehydration tray and dry for another hour or so until completely dry. Store in a sealed container.

BASIC CRACKERS

2 cups seed: pumpkin, sesame, sunflower, or any combination
1 cup flax seeds, ground to a fine meal
1 cup (approximately) charged water
1 tablespoon Celtic sea salt

Soak seeds in water to cover for an hour or two. Drain, rinse with fresh water, and discard soak water. Grind soaked seeds into dough in a food processor, adding water to blend if needed. Or, slowly feed through champion juicer.

Note: Do not run water through the champion; add water after grinding. Add Celtic sea salt and flax seed meal and mix until dough binds.

Press flat onto a dehydrator teflex sheet, and mold into little patties (thick or thin) or bread sticks. Crackers should be about ⅛-inch thick. Garnish with any seed, like poppy or sesame, or chunky Celtic sea salt. Dehydrate at 108°F for 8 hours, flip them over, score them if pressed flat into squares, remove the teflex, and dry for another hour or two until dry. If scored, break into cracker shapes. Store in a sealed container. Will keep for months if properly dried.

CRACKER VARIATIONS

To the Basic Cracker recipe add any of these:

½ cup preferred vegetable—shredded zucchini, chopped red pepper, soaked sun-dried tomato, etc.

¼ cup fresh herbs—parsley, dill, or basil

¼ cup any seed—sesame, flax, sunflower, or poppy

½ cup any soaked nut—walnut, almond, or Brazil

½ cup any dried fruit—raisins, chopped date, or fig

3 tablespoons seasoning—powdered kelp, celery seed, curry powder, or nutritional yeast

1 tablespoon spices—turmeric, black pepper, or cayenne

½ cup soaked whole sea vegetables—hijiki or dulse

CRISPY FLAX CRACKERS

4 garlic cloves, peeled and crushed
1 teaspoon Celtic sea salt, finely ground
3 cups charged water
3 cups flax seed
⅛ cup Bragg Liquid Aminos

Put garlic and Celtic sea salt into the charged water. Add flax seeds and stir well. Soak until all water is absorbed, about 1–2 hours, stirring occasionally. Stir in the Bragg Liquid Aminos and mix well. Let stand for another hour or two, covered at room temperature. With a spoon, spread into thin 3-inch circles on a dehydrator tray using a teflex sheet. These crackers are best when only 2 or 3 flax seeds thick. A too-thick cracker makes for a lot of un-chewed flax seeds. Dehydrate at 108°F. for 6–8 hours then flip and dry other side for 1 more hour.

EGGPLANT JERKY

1 medium eggplant
Charged water, enough to cover eggplant
1 tablespoon Celtic sea salt
2 cups Shoyu soy sauce
¼ tablespoon cayenne powder
½ cup maple syrup, or raw pour able honey
3 tablespoons fresh ginger root, grated, or juiced
Powdered kelp, for garnish
Fresh ground black pepper, to taste

Slice eggplant into ¼-inch thick rounds and lengthwise to create long strips, 2 inches wide. Place eggplant into shallow pans, cover with charged water, and sprinkle one heaping tablespoon of Celtic sea salt. Stir it around, then let soak for 2–3 hours, then drain. Blend remaining ingredients, except kelp and pepper, in shaking jar. Cover eggplant with marinade and toss it well. Let marinate, covered at room temperature, for a few hours. Drain and lay eggplant out on a dehydrator tray with teflex sheet. Sprinkle a light dusting of kelp and pepper to taste, and dehydrate at 108°F for 10–15 hours until tops are dry. Flip, remove teflex, and dry another hour.

LISCIOUS SNACKS

    1 cup pumpkin seeds
    1 cup sunflower seeds
    ½ cup almonds
    1 red bell pepper, deseeded and chopped
    1 small carrot, shredded
    ¼ cup mild onion, chopped
    3 garlic cloves, peeled and crushed
    ½ cup raisins, soaked 20 minutes in ½ cup water
    ½ cup herbs (parsley or cilantro), loosely packed
    2 tablespoons ginger root, grated
    ¼ cup Shoyu soy sauce
    Nori seaweed sheets for rolling

Make a pâté by soaking the pumpkin, sunflower seed, and almonds for 2–3 hours. Drain, rinse well, and discard the soak water. Grind all ingredients, except for the nori sheets, in a food processor. Add a little water to make blending easy if you need to. Make sure to keep the pâté relatively dry.

Cut the nori seaweed sheets into 4 lengthwise strips, a bit bigger than 1 inch wide each. Put pâté into a pastry bag with a wide round nozzle, or make your own pastry bag using a heavy-duty plastic Ziploc freezer bag. Snip off the corner, about ¼ inch, with scissors.

Squeeze a long "drinking-straw" size of pâté onto one side of a length of the nori sheet, and then roll it up—cigar style. Seal the edge of the nori paper by wetting your fingers in a small bowl of water.

Roll it over the seam to seal it. Dehydrate in food dehydrator at 118°F for about 18 hours. Roll them over and dry on other side about an hour or two. They are good when still chewy and moist. Store in sealed plastic out or in the refrigerator.

These snacks are so delicious, everyone will love them. Since they are dehydrated, they'll last for months. Try other pâtés like *Teriyaki Pâté,* or *Hot Curry Pâté* (see recipes, p. 111).

SWEET CURRY LISCIOUS

10 sun-dried tomatoes
Charged water for soaking
1 cup sunflower seeds
½ cup pumpkin seeds
1 cup walnuts
4 medium cucumbers
4 tablespoons unpasteurized miso
1 whole bunch fresh basil
4 tablespoons Shoyu soy sauce
4 tablespoons apple cider vinegar
¼ cup cold-pressed olive oil, or liquid coconut butter
¼ cup spirulina flakes
3 tablespoons curry powder, hot or mild
⅓ cup raw honey
Nori seaweed sheets

Soak sun-dried tomatoes, in water to cover for 2 or 3 hours, until soft. Save the tomato soak water. Separately soak sunflower and pumpkin seed same amount of time. Drain, then rinse well with fresh water. Discard seed soak water. Put tomatoes and their soak water, the drained and rinsed seeds, and all the other ingredients into food processor, using the "S" blade and grind to a chunky paste.

Cut nori sheets into four equal quarters. Squeeze a long "drinking-straw" size of pâté onto one side of a length of the nori sheet, and then roll it up—cigar style. Seal the edge of the nori paper by wetting your fingers in a small bowl of water. Roll it over the seam to seal it. Dehydrate in food dehydrator at 118°F for about 18 hours. Roll them over and dry on other side about an hour or two. They are good when still chewy and moist. Store in sealed plastic out or in the refrigerator.

HOT & SPICY PUMPKIN SEEDS

3 cups raw pumpkin seeds,
Charged water for soaking
1 tablespoon garlic powder (or more to taste)
½ teaspoon cayenne powder
Dash Bragg Liquid Aminos

Soak pumpkin seeds in water 1–2 hours, discard water, and rinse well.
Combine remaining ingredients in a bowl and toss well. Let sit at room
temperature 1 hour, and then toss again. Spread evenly on a teflex dehydrator sheet. Dehydrate at 118°F for several hours until dry on top. Flip
them over and dry for another hour. Allow to cool, then store in a sealed
container. This is a great food for traveling.

*Secret Teaching: We get vital hormones from seeds. Seeds are a wonderful
source of B Vitamins, many minerals, and a good source of essential
fatty acids. Pumpkin seed also contains chlorophyll.*

*Green is clean! An excellent source of tryptophane, and other amino acids,
pumpkin seed also has a gene-repairing and anti-tumor effect (amigdalyn).*

*Pumpkin seeds are loaded with zinc, which is a mood elevator and is involved
in many enzyme systems especially the digestive juices. Zinc enhances smell
and taste and is very important for production of semen and sexual fluid.
Warts, acne, and skin conditions are improved enormously when you consume more zinc.*

SUMMER SQUASH CAKE

2 cups almonds
½ cup flax seed, ground to a meal
1 cup sweet squash, butternut, or zucchini, finely grated
1 ½ tablespoons cinnamon powder
1 teaspoon allspice powder
4 tablespoons molasses
½ cup chopped and pitted dates, soaked for 15 minutes
½ cup charged water for soaking
4 tablespoons maple syrup, or raw honey
1 cup charged water
½ cup raisins
½ cup walnuts, chopped
½ cup coconut, shredded

Soak almonds in charged water to cover for 1 hour, then drain and rinse well with fresh water. Discard soak water. Grind almonds well in food processor with enough water to make a loose batter (about ½ cup). Add a few tablespoons more charged water and the remaining ingredients, except raisins, walnuts, and shredded coconut. Stir raisins and walnuts (whole) into batter. Knead together well until dough binds, then form into one or two small cakes, about 1-inch thick.

Place on teflex dehydrator sheet or waxed paper. Press shredded coconut onto outside of cake. Dehydrate at 118°F for 10–15 hours, then flip over and dry another hour or two.

ORANGE RAISIN BREAD

½ cup walnuts, soaked
½ cup sunflower seeds, soaked
Charged water for soaking
1 cup flax seed meal, ground
5 large soft dates, pitted
1 tablespoon cinnamon
½ teaspoon nutmeg
1 cup orange juice, fresh-squeezed
1 cup raisins
½ cup walnuts, unsoaked and chopped

Soak ½ cup walnuts with sunflower seeds in water to cover for ½ hour. Drain and rinse with fresh water. Discard soak water. Mix all ingredients, except raisins and unsoaked chopped walnuts, together in a food processor using the "S" blade. Stir in raisins and chopped walnuts and mix until dough binds. Press into one or more small cakes. Dehydrate at 118°F for 10–15 hours, then flip over and dry another hour or two.

> NOTE: *The smoother the batter, the softer the bread; so blend until you achieve a smooth consistency.*

ALMOND FIG COOKIES

1 cup almonds, soaked for several hours, drained and rinsed
1 cup walnuts
½ cup sunflower seed, soaked 1 hour, drained and rinsed
8 fresh figs, chopped
½ cup raw honey
¼ cup molasses (optional)
1 tablespoon cinnamon
½ teaspoon nutmeg
Pinch Celtic sea salt
½ cup coconut flakes
1 cup raisins (with seeds)

Soak almonds, then drain and rinse. Grind walnuts to a powder in a blender or food processor. Mix and grind all remaining ingredients, except raisins, in a food processor using the "S" blade. Transfer to a bowl and stir in raisins. Roll into small balls and press flat into cookies onto dehydration rack, using a teflex sheet. Dehydrate at 118°F for 8–10 hours, then flip over, removing the teflex sheet, and dry 1–3 more hours, until dry. Stores well refrigerated for several weeks.

CAROB MINT CANOLIS

5 ripe bananas
1 cup almonds, soaked 1 hour, drained and rinsed
1 cup charged water
1 cup raw carob powder
15 drops peppermint oil, or 1 tablespoon dry peppermint leaf
    from a tea bag or loose tea
2 tablespoons coconut butter
Pinch Celtic sea salt

½ cup shredded coconut

1 tablespoon cinnamon

3 tablespoons raw almonds, unsoaked and chopped

Blend bananas, soaked almonds, and water in a food processor until smooth. Slowly add the carob powder, peppermint oil, coconut butter, and Celtic sea salt and blend well. Pour onto teflex sheets on dehydrator rack and spread into a ¼-inch thick square to the corners of the teflex sheets.

Garnish by sprinkling on cinnamon and carob powder, shredded coconut, and chopped almonds. Gently press garnishes into batter.

Dehydrate for 18 hours at 118°F, until firm. Peel them off the teflex and cut with scissors into 3-inch squares. Roll them into canoli shells by overlapping two pointed corners and securing them with a toothpick. Remember that garnish side goes on the outside of the shell. Dehydrate for 3 more hours on the screened tray, without the teflex sheets. Using a pastry bag, fill with *Vanilla Maple Crème* filling (see recipe, p. 147). Using the big star tip will add a finished look. Don't have a pastry bag? Fill a heavy-duty freezer Ziploc bag and snip off one corner (about ¼ inch) with scissors. Sprinkle a little carob powder over the canolis as an extra touch if you like. Store sealed in the refrigerator, or freeze to keep longer.

NOTE: This recipe includes banana, a fast-moving sugar. This is a special treat for holidays and children.

PIÑA COLATA COOKIES

    4 fat figs, dried or fresh
    1 cup raisins
    1 cup charged water
    4 cups ripe juicy organic pineapple, in chunks
    2 tablespoons raw honey
    2 cups sunflower seeds soaked for 1 hour, drained and rinsed
    2 cups walnuts
    1 cup raw almond butter
    1 cup fresh juice (apple, papaya, or nut milk)
    ½ cup shredded coconut

Soak figs and raisins in 1 cup charged water for 20 minutes, then drain and rinse. Put all ingredients (including half the fig/raisin soak water), except shredded coconut, into a food processor using the "S" blade until well blended. Roll into cookie size balls and then roll in shredded coconut. Chill in refrigerator for 8 hours. They are delicious as refrigerator cookies, or dehydrate them by pressing them flat and drying at 108°F until dry, 5 hours or so. Flip and dry the other side 1 hour.

VANILLA MAPLE CRÈME

  2 cups soft white nuts (skinless macadamia, cashew, almond, etc.), or
     a darker nut for a brown crème
  ¼ cup maple syrup, or honey, date sugar, etc.
  ½ tablespoon pure vanilla extract, without alcohol if you can find it,
     or ½ tablespoon vanilla bean, soaked 1 hour in water
  1 tablespoon lecithin granules
  ¼ cup charged water

Soak nuts in water for 2 or 3 hours (more for almonds, less for cashews and macadamia nuts). Drain, rinse well, and discard the soak water. Blend all ingredients in blender or food processor until smooth.

This crème is a lovely white and contrasts the dark canoli shells nicely. You can play with the color of your crème. Make it bright yellow by adding ¼ teaspoon turmeric, or go crimson red by blending in a thin slice of beet. Play with the flavor by adding a few drops of essential oil, like orange or tangerine, and garnish your crème with long festive curls of orange and or lemon zest.

SPICE CAKE

1 cup hazelnuts
1 cup sunflower seeds
1 cup walnuts
Charged water for soaking
1 cup dried figs
1 cup raisins
2 tablespoons cinnamon
½ teaspoon nutmeg
2 tablespoons lecithin, granules or liquid
¼ cup honey
½ teaspoon cardamom
½ teaspoon Celtic sea salt
1 lemon, juiced
3 tablespoons orange peel, grated
1 teaspoon clove
1 cup pineapple chunks with juice
1 cup chopped walnuts, unsoaked
1 cup shredded coconut
Coconut oil for greasing

Soak hazelnuts, sunflower seeds, and walnuts for ½ hour; then drain well and discard soak water. Grind to a moist meal in a food processor using "S" blade. Set this mixture aside. Soak figs and raisins in charged water for ½ hour. Reserve the soak water and combine figs, raisins, lecithin, honey, cinnamon, nutmeg, cardamom, Celtic sea salt, lemon juice, orange peel, clove, and pineapple chunks in a blender or using a food processor. Remove blended mixture and fold into the set-aside nut/seed meal. Add the unsoaked chopped walnut and shredded coconut. Stir to blend.

Spice Cake should be so very sweet!! Dehydrating it will make it much less tasty, so make sure it is sweet enough to compete with bakery cakes! Grease 2 shallow pans with coconut oil. Fill with batter so that the cake is about 1 inch deep. Dehydrate at 118°F for 24 hours, or until dry and pulled away from the sides. Pop it out of the pan and dehydrate the other side for another hour or two. When cooled, frost with *Vanilla Glaze* (recipe below).

VANILLA GLAZE

> 3 cups macadamia nuts and cashews combined, soaked 15 minutes, drained and rinsed.
> ½ cup maple syrup, or raw honey
> 2 tablespoons vanilla extract
> 2 tablespoons coconut butter

Soak the macadamia nuts and cashews. Drain, rinse, and discard soak water. Blend all ingredients well on high until light and fluffy. Spread on the *Spice Cake* and enjoy!

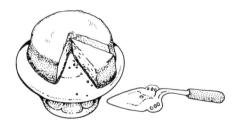

CHAPTER 5

NUT & SEED SPECIALS

Nuts and seeds provide essential fatty acids, complex protein combinations, and a stick-to-your-ribs hearty addition to every meal.

Add raw nutbutter to your smoothie or soup. Grind fresh sesame or pumpkin seed and sprinkle generously over your salad. Seeds provide many hormone ranges that are easily assimilated when the seed is soaked, sprouted, or when the raw seed is ground into a fresh meal. These hormone ranges are broad bases in which other hormones can be made—on the spot and as required by the body.

Nuts can be hard to digest in that they can be difficult to chew well. If you find nuts to be indigestible, begin by taking them first as a nut milk (see recipe in Chapter 7: *Beverages*), then grind, soak, and sprout your favorite nuts.

NUT OR SEED BUTTER

   1 cup raw nut or seed: choose almond, Brazil nut, pine nut, hazel
      nut, pumpkin seed, or sesame seed (see *Raw Sesame Tahini,* recipe
      below)
   5–6 tablespoon charged water
   Pinch Celtic sea salt
   1 tablespoon cold-pressed oil (optional)

Grind nut or seed to a moist fine meal. Mix all ingredients to form a
stiff butter. Use immediately, or store in a sealed container in the refrigerator.

RAW SESAME TAHINI

   1 cup raw sesame seed, un-hulled if possible
   5–7 tablespoon charged water
   Pinch Celtic sea salt

Grind seeds to a moist meal in your coffee grinder. Transfer to a bowl
and mix in water and salt to get a creamy, thick paste. Store in a sealed
container in the refrigerator.

   We make fresh on-the-spot tahini for recipes that call for it by adding
freshly ground sesame seed meal and a few tablespoons of extra water.
Try this in your blender recipes, such as soup or dressing. This really
adds a fresh sesame taste.

*Secret Teaching: Un-hulled sesame seeds contain an enormous amount of
organic calcium. Sesame seeds lose ⅔ of their calcium in the hulling
process.*

NUT OR SEED CHEESE

> 2 cups almonds, sunflower seeds, or pumpkin seeds, soaked for 4
>   hours, drained and rinsed, or ground flax seeds, unsoaked
> 2 cups charged water
> ½ tablespoon Celtic sea salt
> 3 capsules bifitus bulgarious, S-thermaphullus, L-salivarius, or kyo-
>   dophilus

Place all ingredients into blender, empty bacteria capsules and discard empty capsule shell. You can easily find one of these bacteria in your health food store, usually refrigerated. Blend in blender until creamy (liquefied). Pour into glass dish so the mixture about 1½ inches deep. Cover with a towel. Let sit 8–12 hours in warm place (80°F) until it achieves desired tartness. (The top of the refrigerator is a good spot.)

Cheese becomes sharper with more time. For a mild cheese, let sit 8 hours; for a sharper cheese let sit for 12 hours. Then place it in the refrigerator for 2 hours. Transfer to cheesecloth and strain off whey by squeezing. Make a ball of cheese in the cheesecloth and squeeze all excess water out. Keep it in the cheesecloth and leave a bit at the ends so it can be hung. Hang the bag up in the kitchen, over the sink or a container to catch excess draining. Dry for about a day; the dryer the better. Then store in the refrigerator until ready to eat. Cheese is best tasting after it's been refrigerated for 4–6 days. It will keep in fridge for several weeks. This is great on crackers or as a side dish to any plate.

Secret Teaching: Seed cheese, and all ferments, can be viewed as fast foods for friendly intestinal flora (succrolego peptides). It is very important to have some ferments in the diet for rapid and efficient digestion.

BUGS-ON-A-LOG

Celery stalks
Raw nut or seed butter, like almond butter
Raisins

Wash celery. Smear nutbutter onto celery and top with raisins. Great additions to any plate. Kids love them as snacks.

EXOTIC WALNUT PÂTÉ

½ pound feta cheese
4 tablespoons olive oil
½–⅔ cup nut milk, strained
2 cups raw walnuts, chopped
1 teaspoon paprika
Cayenne pepper, to taste

Rinse salt brine off the feta and place in the blender along with 2 table-spoons of olive oil, all called for nut milk, and ⅔ cup of walnuts. Blend down to chunks by pulsing. Add the remaining ingredients while blending on a medium speed into a smooth paste. Chill in the refrigerator. This is good on bread, cucumber rounds, crackers, and as a vegetable dip. Keeps well in refrigerator for days. Great party dip.

> NOTE: Feta cheese makes this a non-vegan dish, and raw feta is hard to find. Yet, it's so delicious and appropriate for the person still eating cheese who is yet to become 100% LifeFood. Great party food.

WILD MANITOK RICE SALAD

½ pound wild Canadian rice (actually a wild-harvested grass seed)
water for soaking
½ cup sweet onion, chopped
½ cup zucchini or carrot, shredded
½ cup red bell pepper, deseeded and chopped
1 handful Chinese bean sprouts
1 stalk broccoli tops, skin and dice the stem

Soak the wild rice for 8 hours, drain and rinse well. Sprout for 2 days, rinsing 3 times daily and draining well. In a large bowl combine sprouted wild rice and vegetables. (Be creative and choose vegetables you have on hand.) Choose a sauce, dressing, or marinade from Chapter 3 and toss 1 cup or more with the rice salad. This is a very special dish! It will win anyone over to LifeFood.

This rice is actually a seed that is hand-harvested by the Manitok Indians of the Great Lakes region. Easy to digest and an important bodybuilding dish, this will easily become a regular on your menu. This special dish satisfies in the way cooked grain dishes used to. We like to keep the plain sprouted rice in the refrigerator to toss over salads or to fill an avocado half and add some oil and salt.

DINNER GRAINS

Choose several grains, such as amaranth, quinoa, kamut, oat groats, barley, millet, wheat, etc.

½ cup charged water
Celtic sea salt, to taste

Soak 1 or 2 cups grain overnight and sprout for 2 days, rinsing 3 times daily, until soft. Take ⅔ of the sprouted grain and grind in food processor with charged water. Then mix with remaining whole grain sprouts. Serve as is, or warmed a little over low heat for a few minutes. Add Celtic sea salt to taste. Serve as a side dish with: *Peanut Garlic Shredded Salad, Spicy Ginger Shiitake,* or *Teriyaki Vegetables* (see recipes, pp. 93, 101, & 104).

CHAPTER 6

FRUIT MEALS & DESSERT

RED CLOUD DRINK

    3 large red delicious apples
    3 medium Asian pears
    15 strawberries
    ½ medium papaya, peeled, wrapped in plastic and frozen a day
        or more
    1 mango, peeled and pitted

Juice together the apples, pears, and strawberries. Blend the papaya
and mango in a blender and add to the already juiced fruit. Makes small
pitcher of gorgeous beverage.

WATERMELON ICE SORBET

> 1 organic watermelon, rind cut off and melon deseeded
> ¼ cup lemon or lime juice
> Charged water
> Mint leaf and lemon curls to garnish

Remove watermelon seeds and dark green outer rind and discard. Fill blender with watermelon, lemon or lime juice, and some charged water to liquefy. Freeze the juice in shallow pans, or ice cube trays, for 6 or 7 hours until frozen well. Remove from pans and break into pieces. Blend well in blender. Add charged water to whip to a thick sorbet consistency. Scoop into glass sorbet bowls. Garnish with mint leaf and lemon curl. Serve immediately.

Be sure to avoid the seedless craze and buy only organic watermelon with seeds—the way nature made them. Seedless fruits are highly hybridized to make them sterile. Sterile food has a lower vibration and must be sprayed with many chemicals to be seedless. Eat fertile foods, and become more fertile yourself!

SUPER SIMPLE SMOOTHIE

> 4 cups grapefruit juice   1 basket blueberries

Blend until smooth. Add ice cubes (made with charged water) to make it a chilled cooler. Use any juice with any fruit for variety.

CHERRY PAPAYA SMOOTHIE

> 2 cups frozen black cherries, pitted
> 1 cup papaya, skinned, seeded
> 1 small avocado, or ½ large avocado
> 1 heaping tablespoon lecithin granules
> 4 cups nut milk (see recipes, pp. 197, 198, or 199)

Blend well. This simple smoothie has endless variations.

CLASSIC SMOOTHIE

    1½ cups favorite berries, fresh or frozen

    ½ avocado, or 2 pears, cored

    ½ blender of fresh, raw apple cider, or 3–4 cups any raw fruit juice, or
        nut milk

    ¼ cup flax seed

    1 tablespoon lecithin, liquid or granules

    2 tablespoons flax seed oil

Add berries, fresh or frozen, and avocado (or pear) and fill blender to half full with apple cider. Grind flax seed in coffee grinder and add to blender with lecithin and flax seed oil, mixing all other ingredients in a blender on high speed for a few minutes until whipped and frothy. For a thicker smoothie add more fruit or flax seed. For a thinner smoothie add more juice or nut milk.

CHERRY NUT MILK SMOOTHIE

    2 cups frozen black cherries, pitted (okay to substitute blueberries)

    ½–1 cup fruit (apple, pear, peach, or combination)

    4 cups nut milk

    1 heaping tablespoon lecithin granules

    3 tablespoons flax seed oil, or coconut oil

    2 tablespoon bee pollen

    1 tablespoon spirulina flakes with lecithin, or any blue green algae

    ¼ tablespoon vanilla extract (non-alcohol is always best)

    ¼ cup fresh ground flax meal (optional)

    2 tablespoon raw honey

    Pinch Celtic sea salt

Blend all ingredients well.

Secret Teaching: This smoothie is good for sugar-sensitive people as the fruits are balanced nicely with the protein and fat of the nut milk and oils.

SUPER SMOOTHIE

½ blender of fresh, raw apple cider, or nut milk
¼ cup flax seed, ground to a fine meal
1 teaspoon cinnamon
1½ cups berries: blueberries, blackberries, cherries, or raspberries
1 avocado, or, 2 pears, cored
1 heaping tablespoon spirulina, or blue green algae
3 heaping tablespoons fresh bee pollen
1 tablespoon lecithin liquid, or granules
3 tablespoons flax seed oil, or coconut butter
1 tablespoon raw honey (optional)
Pinch Celtic sea salt

Fill blender half full with apple cider, or nut milk. Grind flax seed with cinnamon in coffee grinder and add to blender. Add all other ingredients and turn blender on low until the mixture is moving smoothly. Then blend well on high for 2 minutes until creamy.

A meal for 2, or a snack for 4.

Secret Teaching: This smoothie is a high-protein meal, containing both bee pollen and spirulina, which are two of the highest quality sources of protein on the planet! They both contain very long chains of amino acids that break down easily to single amino acids for maximum protein assimilation.

160

Flax seed and berries provide five different types of fiber: cellulose, hemicellulose, gums, lignin, and fruit fiber—all good for chelating radioactive isotopes out of the body, maintaining the youthfulness of the body. Lecithin and flax seed oil combine to cause the body to produce high-density lipoproteins that are essential in helping the liver manage fats.

The carotenoids and the selenium in the Spirulina help protect immune cells (phagocytes) from auto-oxidative damage, and enhance T- and B-lymphocyte proliferative response. This enhances cytotoxic immunity.

DYNAMITE SMOOTHIE VARIATIONS

Be creative with your smoothie. Add any one of these variations to the above recipe and have yourself a delicious treat! Make a meal of it!
- shredded coconut
- soaked raisins, or currants
- pear, apple, peach
- mango, papaya
- orange
- persimmons
- ginseng powder (for men)
- dong quai powdered herb (for woman)

Secret Teaching: You can add extra nutrition to your smoothie by adding whole food vitamin and mineral complex supplements and blend. Grind them to a powder in a coffee grinder and add to smoothie before blending. Add chromium GTF, B-Vitamin complex, folic acid with Vitamin B-12, enzymes, etc. The B Vitamins potentiate your ability to deal with sugars, stress, enhance dream recall, and help heal carpal-tunnel syndrome.

BIG FIG SMOOTHIE

    5 dried figs, soaked, or fresh figs
    Charged water for soaking
    4 cups unpasteurized apple juice
    1 pear, cubed or shredded
    1 mango, ½ avocado, or 1 apple
    ¼ cup ground flax meal
    2 tablespoons flax seed oil or coconut butter

If figs are dried, soak them in charged water to cover for about half an hour, or more. Add all ingredients to blender. Blend on high speed for 3 minutes if you're using dried figs, or 2 minutes if using fresh ones. Dry figs take longer to thoroughly masticate because of the dried hormone-rich seeds. Fresh fig seeds blend more easily.

    A meal for 2, or a snack for 4.

COCONUT RASPBERRY SMOOTHIE

    4 cups Brazil nut milk
    1 apple, cored and cut into chunks
    1 cup raspberries
    ½ avocado
    ¼ cup shredded coconut, fresh if you can get it
    1 handful raisins
    ¼ cup ground flax meal
    3 tablespoons flax seed oil or coconut butter
    2 tablespoons soy lecithin
    Raw honey, liquid stevia herb, or maple syrup, to taste

Blend all ingredients in blender at high speed for 3 minutes.

    Meal for 2, or a snack for 4.

SUPER SWAMP SMOOTHIE

4 cups fresh, raw apple cider, or other fresh raw juice
½ pint blueberries
2 pears, cubed
1 heaping tablespoon blue green algae, or spirulina
3 heaping tablespoons ground flax seed meal
3 tablespoons flax seed oil
2 tablespoons lecithin, granules or liquid
Pinch Celtic sea salt

Blend all ingredients in blender at high speed for 3 minutes.

A meal for 2, or a snack for 4.

Secret Teaching: Spirulina is one of the highest quality sources of protein, coming in at a whopping 60% protein. Flesh is only about 27% protein; legumes tend to have more protein than flesh. Spirulina has all of the essential amino acids. It is the world's highest source of Vitamin B12 with high concentrations of Vitamins A, B1, B2, B6, Vitamin D, E, and K—a significant source of growth factor, lots of chlorophyll, pigments, and ferrodoxins. Spirulina has all the necessary minerals, trace elements, cell salts, and enzymes. It helps curb the appetite and satisfies hunger by offering complete nutrition.

SPIRULINA CHOCOLATE CONFECTION

2 tablespoons raw creamed honey
2 tablespoons spirulina, or blue green algae
2 tablespoons flax seed oil (with borage if possible)
2 tablespoons pumpkin seed butter (or other seed or nutbutter)
2 tablespoons raw powdered carob
Pinch Celtic sea salt

Cream all ingredients together and adjust tastes to your preference. This really satisfies when something sweet is in order.

Makes a single serving, about ¼ cup.

BEE POLLEN & FLAX SEED OIL

3 tablespoons bee pollen (kept fresh in the freezer)
2–3 tablespoons flax seed oil

Mix in a small bowl with a chopstick. Slowly eat the mixture with a little dessert spoon. Makes a meditative dessert or easy nutritional hit to pick you up.

Makes 1 serving.

Secret Teaching: Like spirulina, bee pollen is an excellent source of protein and a great immune system enhancer. It is excellent for protecting us from allergies and brings relief to arthritis. Flax seed oil has colloids in it that are smaller than a wavelength of light. These wavelengths are energized by photons of sunlight, helping to bring electric tension to cell membranes for high cell nutrition permeability.

FRUIT & POLLEN BREAKFAST BOWL

1 apple, diced
1 pear, diced
½ cup raw apple cider
1 handful raisins
1 handful almonds, soaked 1 hour, drained and rinsed
1 handful sunflower seeds, soaked 1 hour, drained and rinsed
¼ cup shredded coconut
2 heaping tablespoons soft, fresh bee pollen
1 cup fresh juice

Place apple, pear, apple cider, raisins, almonds, and sunflower seeds in a single bowl and top with shredded coconut, bee pollen, and a cup of your favorite fresh juice.

A nutritious and delicious breakfast or snack for 1.

APPLE SUNFLOWER CREAM

1 large tangy apple, peeled and cut into pieces
1 cup sunflower seeds, soaked 3 hours, rinsed and drained
½ cup charged water, or apple juice
Pinch Celtic sea salt

Add the apple to blender with sunflower seeds and charged water, or apple juice. Add salt and blend into a stiff cream. Wonderful as a topping to fruit bowls or simply spoon it up as is!

PHAT BLACK SORBET

    1 cup blackberries or blueberries, frozen
    1 cup cherries, frozen
    1 tablespoon spirulina flakes w/lecithin
    ½ cup fresh juice (enough to blend)
    Raw honey, liquid stevia herb, or maple syrup, to taste
    Pinch Celtic sea salt

Blend all ingredients well to crush seeds in berries; pulse first, then blend on high speed to grind seed thoroughly.

    Serves 2 or 3.

> *NOTE: This becomes a super nutrition treat by blending in some whole food vitamin and mineral supplements, like 1 or 2 tabs of chromium.*

RASPBERRY CHIFFON SORBET

    2–3 tablespoons raw honey or maple syrup, or a few drops liquid
        stevia herb, to taste
    ½ cup orange juice, fresh-squeezed
    3 cups raspberries, frozen
    1 heaping tablespoon lecithin granules
    1 tablespoon orange peel, grated
    Pinch Celtic sea salt
    6 ice cubes (for desired thickness)

Blend raw honey (or liquid stevia herb or honey) and orange juice in blender. Add remaining ingredients and blend well. Add ice cubes or chips to make a thicker sorbet. Blend very well so that the precious hormones contained within the tiny seeds of the berry become available to us. Blend until you stop hearing the seed being split! A special treat is to make ice cubes out of raw juice. Use those and you'll have a very flavorful sorbet.

Makes about 4 servings.

SUNSHINE PUDDING

2 tablespoons raw honey
2 tablespoons flax seed oil or coconut butter
10 drops of bee propolys
10 drops of Christopher's pine elixir (optional)
3 tablespoons Jubbs TOCOtreinols Powder (optional)
1 tablespoon charged water
1 tablespoon bee pollen
Berries to garnish

Mix all ingredients with wood a spoon (except for bee pollen, water, and berries) into a thick base, and then add water until smooth and creamy. Sprinkle with bee pollen, garnish with berries, chill, and serve. TOCOtreinols Powder is a delicious Vitamin E grown on rice bran so it is a sweet powder. It has amazing anti-oxidant properties and is approximately 200 times more potent than ordinary vitamin E.

A snack for 1.

CREAMY MANGO SORBET

1 pound mango, peeled, pitted, and frozen
6 ice cubes
Fresh-squeezed juice, coconut water, or charged water

Once the mango is peeled and pitted, seal it in a plastic bag and freeze 1–2 days. Blend mango with a few ice cubes in blender; add a few ounces of fresh fruit juice, coconut water, or charged water to blend. Adjust thickness by adding more or less juice. It has the consistency and texture of ice cream! If you prefer, skip the ice and just run frozen mango through a champion juicer with the homogenizer plate in for a Mango Ice Cream. Also, try adding other frozen fruit like peach, berries, or apricots for flavor and color varieties.

Makes about 2–3 servings.

ALMOND VANILLA SORBET

2 cups almonds soaked for 3 hours, skins peeled off
2 cups charged water
2 golden delicious apples, cored and peeled
3 tablespoons liquid lecithin
1 vanilla bean, or 2 tablespoons vanilla extract
Raw honey, liquid stevia herb, or maple syrup, to taste
Pinch Celtic sea salt

Blend all ingredients and freeze in shallow pans. Break into pieces and blend in blender or Champion Juicer.

ALMOND PRUNE BALLS

1 pound soft dried prunes, pitted, chopped, and soaked in charged
   water for an hour
1 cup charged water, for soaking
1½ cups soaked almonds
1 cup shredded coconut
½ tablespoon almond extract
Pinch Celtic sea salt
Whole almonds, to garnish

Soak almonds for approximately an hour, then drain and rinse for an
hour. Discard almond soak water. Soak prunes for an hour and reserve
the soak water. Put prunes with their soak water in food processor or
blender and cut to a chunky meal. Blend almond meal with prunes and
soak water together. Blend to a paste. In a bowl, combine almond meal,
prune paste, almond extract, salt, and half the shredded coconut. Mix
well. Spoon it up and roll into balls. Roll the balls in the remaining
shredded coconut and press a whole almond onto the top.

FRUIT SALAD WITH CINNAMON RAISIN SAUCE

    4 apples, cored and diced
    4 cups strawberries, diced
    3 pears, diced
    1½ cups papaya, peeled, deseeded, and diced
    2 peaches or nectarines (whatever is in season), diced
    2 oranges, diced
    2 cups fresh raw apple juice
    1 cup raisins or dried figs
    1 cup shredded coconut
    1 teaspoon cinnamon
    1 tablespoon ginger
    1 teaspoon allspice
    1 teaspoon clove

Place the diced fruit in a large bowl. Blend remaining ingredients for
30 seconds so that the mixture is still a little chunky. Pour sauce over
fruit salad and toss well. Garnish with additional shredded coconut.
For nut lovers, soak 1 cup raw almond or sunflower seed for 1–2 hours.
Chop almonds with a large knife on a cutting board and toss onto salad.

    Makes about 4 servings.

STUFFED FIGS

    10 dry figs
    ¼ cup shredded or ground coconut
    10 teaspoons raw almond butter
    10 whole pecans

Split pitted figs and fill with nutbutter. Roll in coconut and press pecan
on top. Makes 10 rich and sweet treats.

BROWNIES

⅔ cup flax seed, ground to a moist meal

2 cups raw carob

1 tablespoon cinnamon

1 teaspoon Celtic sea salt

⅓ cup coconut butter

1 tablespoon vanilla extract

1 cup charged water

⅔ cup maple syrup, or raw honey

10 large dried figs

Grind dry flax seeds to a moist meal in blender or grinder. Put seed meal along with remaining ingredients into the food processor, using the "S" blade. A good blender can do the job, too. If using honey rather than maple syrup, warm the honey in the 1 cup of water, just enough to dissolve it, then blend well. Pour into shallow pan and dehydrate at 118°F for 24 hours. Try adding ½ cup chopped walnuts to the batter or top the brownies with them. Frost with *Wicked Frosting* (see recipe, p. 173).

CAROB NUT LOG

1 cup almonds, soaked 1 hour, drained and rinsed

2 cups sunflower seeds, soaked 1 hour, drained and rinsed

1 cup raisins, soaked in 1 cup charged water (reserve the water for
  frosting)

1 cup walnuts

1 cup raw carob powder

Shredded coconut, to garnish

In a food processor, grind the soaked almond, sunflower seed, and raisins. Add a little charged water to keep it moving. As it becomes smooth, add remaining ingredients. Add more carob if you like, and adjust the sweetness to your preference. Add chopped nuts if you like. On a flat plate roll the mixture so it binds and make a log. Frost with *Wicked Frosting* (see recipe, p. 173). Garnish with shredded coconut.

BASIC FROSTING

1 cup white nut or seed, soaked (such as almond, macadamia, pine,
  Brazil)

½ cup raisins, honey, or maple syrup

1 cup charged water, juice, or nut milk

¼ cup Orange, lemon, raw carob, fresh or frozen berries, vanilla
  extract, to flavor

1 teaspoon beet juice powder, or turmeric powder, to color

Pinch Celtic sea salt

Add 1 tablespoon of lecithin granules to make it creamy (optional)

Soak for a few hours, then drain and rinse seed/nuts, add salt, then chop them up in the blender. This serves as your base. Blend in raisins, honey, or maple syrup to sweeten. Add charged water or juice or nut milk to adjust thickness. Flavor and color your frosting with the ingredients of your choice.

WICKED FROSTING

    1 cup raisins, soaked
    1 cup charged water, for soaking
    1 avocado
    3 tablespoons honey or maple syrup to taste (optional)
    1 teaspoon pure vanilla extract
    ½ cup raw carob powder, or more to taste

Soak the raisins in charged water for one hour. Reserve the soak water. Using the "S" blade on your food processor, blend avocado, water, and honey. Then add vanilla extract, and carob powder last and gradually. Adjust sweetness to your preference. Frost *Brownies* or *Carob Nut Log* (see recipes, pp. 171 & 172) with this frosting. It looks and tastes great with flaked coconut.

ORANGE FIG FROSTING

    4 large fresh figs, or dried figs, soaked in charged water (reserve
       water)
    Charged water, for soaking
    1 cup sunflower seed, soaked, drained, and rinsed
    ½ cup orange juice, fresh-squeezed
    2 tablespoons orange peel
    1 tablespoons lecithin granules

Use fresh figs if you can. If not, soak dried figs for an hour or two in water to cover them. Save soak water and add both the water and figs to blender. Blend all ingredients well in blender. Add more juice or soak water for thinner glaze-like frosting. Add less juice for a thicker frosting. Try substituting almonds for sunflower seed, peel off hull after soaking. Almonds require soaking 2–3 hours to loosen hull. Or choose any soft nut or seed, including macadamia, walnut, pine nut, or Brazil nut.

    Yields 1½ cups.

RADIANT RUBY FROSTING

> 1 cup fatty nut, like macadamia, pine nut, or Brazil nut, soaked in
> charged water to cover
> ½ cup beet juice
> ½ cup maple syrup
> 1 whole avocado, peeled and pitted
> 1 teaspoon vanilla extract

Soak nuts for 1 hour. Drain and rinse. Discard soak water. Blend all
ingredients in food processor or blender. This frosting is a beautiful
shade of red. Make a fruit faux fondue with tart green apple slices and
chunks of fruit served with this frosting as a dip.

FLUFFY CAROB FROSTING

> 1 cup raw carob powder
> 1 ripe avocado
> 1 cup macadamia nuts, or walnuts
> 1 tablespoon liquid lecithin
> ½ cup maple syrup

Blend all ingredients well in blender. Frost dehydrated cookies, Carob
Nut Log, or make a parfait- alternate fresh berries and frosting in a tall
narrow glass.

> Makes about 3 cups.

CRIMSON MACADAMIA CRÈME

2 cups raw macadamia nuts
5 large dates, pitted
1 cup charged water
¼ cup maple syrup
2 thin slices beet

Soak macadamia nuts and pitted dates in approximately 1 cup water 20 minutes to soften. Toss all ingredients into blender and whip to a creamy smooth texture. Add another beet slice for a darker color.

For variety you can try not soaking the nuts. Blend it so some little chunks remain. This is a gorgeous ruby-colored dressing. Great as icing on a cake or pie! Frost cookies and sprinkle flakes of coconut. This crème is great for making a simple fruit bowl special. It only takes a few minutes to make. We use dates here, something we do rarely in LifeFood nutrition. Dates are high glycemic foods and can be substituted with dried figs for the sugar sensitive person.

Makes about 2½ cups.

LIVE APPLE PIE

½ cup shredded coconut, more if desired for garnishing
1 cup walnuts, ground
1 cup pitted dates, soaked in water to cover for 15 minutes
½ cup soaked sunflower seed, soaked 20 minutes, drained and rinsed
4 cups shredded apples
2½ teaspoons cinnamon
½ cup apple juice
⅔ cup raisins, or dried figs, or prunes

Mix together the shredded coconut, walnuts, pitted dates, and sunflower seeds in the food processor and press it out into a pie shell to form your crust. Set aside. Grate enough apples to fill an oblong cake pan generously, about 4 cups, and place them in a large mixing bowl. Add cinnamon, apple juice, and raisins together and blend. Stir the blended mixture into the bowl of grated apples and mix thoroughly. Fill the pie crust with the apple filling. Garnish with more shredded coconut. Serve or refrigerate. This is a delicious fruit meal or festive gathering dessert. Bring this pie to a potluck dinner and entice your friends to the Life-Food diet! Keeps well covered in refrigerator for 2 days.

Serves 8–10.

SWEET POTATO PIE

2 cups walnuts

½ cup coconut meat

6 large dried figs, soaked and drained

½ cup raisins, soaked in 1 cup charged water (reserve soak water)

½ cups coconut meat, fresh soft or shredded

1 tablespoon cinnamon

1 teaspoon nutmeg

1 tablespoon raw honey or maple syrup (optional)

3 medium sweet potatoes, shredded

Grind walnuts, coconut meat, and figs in a food processor with the "S" blade to an almost-creamy texture. Press the crust meal evenly into a pie plate. It's great as is, or dehydrate at 118°F for a few hours for a firmer crust. Set aside and prepare filling. Blend the raisin soak water, coconut meat, cinnamon, nutmeg, and honey in blender. Toss with raisins and shredded sweet potato and fill the dehydrated pie crust. Refrigerate 3 hours.

Makes a nice dessert for 6, or a sweet breakfast for 4.

ALL BERRY PIE

1 cup raw almonds, or ½ cup filbert, soaked 1 hour, drained and rinsed

1 cup sunflower seeds, soaked 1 hour, drained and rinsed

½ cup walnuts, ground (or other high fat nut)

½ cup soft dates, pitted

½ cup raisins

½ teaspoon almond or vanilla extract (optional)

2 cups ripe berries: blueberries, blackberries, raspberries, strawberries

5 soft fresh fat figs, or dry figs, soaked 1 hour

½ Hass avocado

1 teaspoon lemon juice, fresh-squeezed

4 cups fresh berries (note: 6 cups total for the whole pie!)

Grind the nuts and seeds in a food processor. Add in dates, raisins, and almond extract. Blend well. Press into pie shell. Use as is or put into a dehydrator at 118°F for 3 hours for a firmer crust. This comes in handy as you wish to make crusts a day or two ahead to fill on demand. Keep crusts covered and refrigerated for up to a week or frozen for months. Set pie crust aside while you make the binding and filler. For the binder, mix together the ripe berries, figs, avocado, and lemon juice in a blender or food processor. If using dried figs, remove their stems and soak in 1 cup water. Put the sweet soak water in the blender as well. Set aside. The remaining 4 cups of berries should be cleaned and sliced. Pour the binder over the berries and mix well, then fill the pie shell. Decorate by arranging berries on top. Refrigerate for 2 or more hours to set before serving this sensational dish. This dish is also nice as a frozen pie. Cover with plastic wrap and put in freezer. Let frozen pie stand 5 minutes before serving.

FROZEN BERRY FRUIT PIE

1 cup almonds, soaked 1 hour, drained and rinsed

1 cup walnuts, chopped and ground

½ cup sunflower seeds, soaked 1 hour, drained and rinsed

1 cup raisins, soaked 1 hour (reserve soak water)

¼ cup shredded coconut

2 cups fruit chunks (papaya, mango, and peach), frozen

2 cups berries (raspberries, strawberries, or other berries)

3 large dried figs, soaked for1 hour in charged water

½ cup charged water, for soaking

½ cup coconut flakes

4 mangos, peeled, pitted, and frozen in plastic

⅔ cup flax seed, ground to a meal

Fresh berries, sliced for finishing the pie

Shredded coconut, to garnish

Blend nuts and seeds, raisins, and shredded coconut well in food processor until it will bind when pressed. Press into pie shell. Use as is, or dehydrate at 118°F for several hours. Allow to cool, then cover and refrigerate until you're ready to use it. It's always nice to have a few crusts pre-made and ready to go. Make a few now and have them on hand for tomorrow. For the bottom layer of this pie, blend together the frozen fruit chunks, berries, figs with their soak water, and coconut flakes. Fill the pie with this layer and freeze while you prepare the topping. Use the fig soak water to blend if needed. Run the frozen mango (or other fruit) through Champion juicer to make sorbet. Remove the pie that's been in the freezer setting and spread the sorbet evenly over the existing layer. Sprinkle flax meal over top of the sorbet. Garnish with berries and shredded coconut if desired. Cover and freeze several hours until very firm. Thaw 5 minutes before serving if it has been frozen overnight. For a change you may reverse the filling and topping. Put frozen mango "sorbet" layer as the first layer. Then top with the filling and topping. Fresh ground flax seed meal can be sprinkled over mango layer and on top of pie. Garnish heavily with fresh berries and coconut flakes.

CHERRY COBBLER

½ cup dried figs, soaked in charged water to cover for 20 minutes
½ cup raisins, soaked in charged water to cover for 20 minutes
1 cup walnuts
¼ cup shredded coconut
2 cups fruit (your favorite, like berries and cherries, pitted)
2 cups frozen black cherries
1 large Hass avocado
3 tablespoons raw honey or maple syrup, or 5 dates
Soak water from raisins and figs (from above)
1 cup white nut (macadamia or cashew), soaked 20 minute, drained
    and rinsed
4 tablespoons raw honey or maple syrup, or 4 big dates
1 teaspoon vanilla extract
Charged water (just a little) to blend
Shredded coconut, to garnish
Extra fruit, to garnish

Soak raisins and figs in charged water to cover them for 20 minutes. Drain off the soak water and reserve for the binder (a later step). Put with the soaked raisins and figs, along with the walnuts and shredded coconut, into food processor and grind to a chunky meal. Press firmly into a pie shell. Use your crust as is or dehydrate it in a food dehydrator at 118°F for several hours. Fill the pie crust with the 2 cups of fruit of your choosing. Any fruit will do here. Set the fruit in the pie and set aside while you make the binding. In a blender, mix together the 2 cups of frozen black cherries, Hass avocado, raw honey, and soak water left over from the raisins and figs that you reserved from the crust ingredients. Blend well until smooth. Carefully pour the binder over the fruit filling. Give the pie a little shake to settle all the ingredients.

To make a crème to top the cobbler, soak the macadamia nuts for 20 minutes, drain water, and rinse the nuts. Blend the nuts with the honey, vanilla extract, and as much charged water as is needed to achieve a thick crème. Carefully pour crème over the mixture of binder and filling, using a spoon to spread it out evenly and smoothly. Garnish with shredded coconut and extra fruit. Refrigerate several hours to let it set. Will keep for 2 days covered in the refrigerator.

BREAKFAST BOWL

    10 raw almonds, soaked and chopped
    1 apple, cored and cut into bite-sized pieces
    2 slices dried persimmon, sliced long and thin
    1 pear, cored and shredded
    Cinnamon powder

Soak almonds for 20 minutes to 1 hour. Drain and rinse, discarding the soak water. Fill serving-size bowl with chopped apples and sliced persimmons. Finely shred the pear over the top of the fruit chunks. Add the soaked almonds and a sprinkle of cinnamon. This is great as is. The pear acts as the sauce. You can also top this with any LifeFood frosting or crème, like *Cherry Cobbler Crème* (see end of *Cherry Cobbler* recipe, p. 180), *Orange Fig Frosting* (recipe, p. 173), or *Crimson Macadamia Crème* (recipe, p. 175).

ESSENE FRENCH TOAST

 Essene sun seed bread, or Manna brand
 Maple syrup, to taste
 ¼ cup Almond Milk, unstrained and extra sweet
 ½ cup any fruit, sliced
 Fresh figs, to garnish
 Raisins, to garnish
 Shredded coconut, to garnish
 Cinnamon powder, to garnish
 Nutmeg, to garnish

Manna bread is the closest thing to LifeFood bread on the market. Find it in the frozen section of your health food store. Slice and warm the bread under broiler for only a few minutes, until warm. Top with maple syrup and thick, chunky extra sweet *Almond Milk* (see recipe, p. 197). Garnish with fruit, chopped fresh figs, raisins, shredded coconut, and a dash of cinnamon and nutmeg.

BREAD ALTERNATIVES:

 2 cups sprouted quinoa, or other grain
 Good pinch Celtic sea salt
 2 tablespoons coconut butter
 Enough water to make desired consistency

Mix the bread ingredients to get a pasty batter. Form bread into "toast patties" and dehydrate on teflex sheets at 118°F for 8–10 hours. Flip over and dry 1 more hour until dry. Prepare Essene French Toast as described in the original recipe.

MUESLI BUCKWHEATIES

2 cups raw buckwheat

5 cups charged water, for soaking

2 cups raisins, soaked, soak water reserved

1½ cup charged water, for soaking

½ cup raw honey or maple syrup

1 cup sunflower seeds, soaked 1 hour, drained and rinsed

½ cup shredded coconut (optional)

2 heaping tablespoons cinnamon

1 tablespoons nutmeg

Soak buckwheat in 5 cups charged water in a large bowl, covered, overnight. In the morning, drain off any excess water and discard. Soak raisins (manuka are best or another seeded raisin) in 1 ½ cups charged water for 20 minutes to an hour. In a blender blend raisins and their soak water until smooth. Pour over buckwheat and add soaked sunflower seeds, shredded coconut, cinnamon, and nutmeg and toss well.

Spread Buckwheaties mixture onto dehydrator trays using a teflex sheet so it is less than 1-inch thick. Dehydrate at 118°F for 8–10 hours, until the top layer is dry. Flip over onto the screened dehydrator tray, remove the teflex sheet, and dry the other side for an hour, until dry. Once dry, crumble apart. Serve with any seed or nut milk. Store in a sealed container. Keeps well for many weeks or perhaps months. This does not need not to be refrigerated.

Variations: Add any of the following, before or after dehydrating:

- Unsoaked whole raisins or dates
- Chopped nuts or seeds
- Dried fruit—mangoes, apples, or blueberries

This Muesli Buckwheaties recipe has many variations. Kids love it! This gracefully replaces dead dry cereals with cow milk with yummy seed or nut milk. They're much more inexpensive, delicious, and nutritious than cow milk. Have a bowl of Buckwheaties for the Breakfast of Champions!

SOAKED-SEED BREAKFAST BOWL

1 cup combined almonds, pumpkin seeds, sunflower seeds, soaked with charged water to cover
Berries, fresh or frozen, to desired quantity
Apple chunks, to desired quantity
Pear slices, to desired quantity
Raisins, to desired quantity

Soak nuts and seeds for 1 hour in charged water. Drain, rinse, and discard soak water. Either keep whole or pulse grind them in food processor or blender to an "oatmeal" consistency.

If desired, sweeten with honey or soak ¼ cup raisins in charged water for an hour and use the sweetened water (very sweet and yummy!) and raisins on top. Top with spoonfuls of pulpy, thick *Almond Milk* (see recipe, p. 197). Try adding 1 tablespoon of bee pollen or coconut flakes.

This is a filling day-starter for those who work hard physically and need long-lasting energy release. Great for bodybuilders and an excellent breakfast for children.

CHAPTER 7

BEVERAGES

Remember to always have one or more of the following beverages on hand. Have something yummy and ready to drink for the family, or to offer guests. An exciting and delicious beverage can be just the thing to spark an interesting conversation on LifeFood nutrition amongst your friends.

We happen to live in apple country and can get fresh-pressed raw apple cider nearly year round at our farmers market. Remember to make sure it's raw and has no preservatives, and that it comes refrigerated.

Beverages sold in glass containers have a shelf life and are almost always pasteurized (no enzyme life force).

ELECTROLYTE LEMONADE

3 organic lemons, yellow skin removed, white pith intact
3 tablespoons oil: flax, olive, or coconut butter
1 organic pear, cored
1 teaspoon Celtic sea salt
6 cups charged water
6 tablespoons raw honey, maple syrup, or liquid stevia herb, to taste

Blend all ingredients well in blender. A healing and remarkably refreshing beverage. The lemon and oil detoxify while boosting the immune system. Citrus pectin restores absorption of fats. Add other fruits to enhance flavor, such as peach or apple. An excellent beverage for keeping the bowels moving.

Makes 1 pitcher.

This beverage plays an essential role in Jubbs 14-Day LifeFood Nutritional Fast (Gallbladder Flush). See *LifeFood Nutritional Fasting*, Chapter 10.

Secret Teaching: Celtic sea salt is rich in magnesium. You will find magnesium mostly in the sea, with very little on land. Magnesium is used to excrete sodium. As a metal, it is a major activator of enzyme systems. Magnesium helps keep potassium in the cells. It's a great alkalizer. Magnesium is nature's tranquilizer. If your diet consists of simple sugars, refined carbohydrates, fats, starch, and protein, then you need magnesium. Magnesium helps cleave these molecules in the digestive process and allows the body to break them down into assimilable parts. A thinking person uses up to 50% more magnesium than a non-thinking person (couch potato) does.

OLD-FASHIONED LEMONADE

3 lemons, yellow skin removed, white pith intact
½ cup raw clover honey, to taste
6–7 cups charged water, to fill blender

Blend all ingredients well on medium, then high for 2 minutes until frothy and foamy. Keeps refrigerated for several days.

Makes 1 pitcher.

PEACH LEMONADE COOLER

¾ blender of *Old-Fashioned Lemonade* (see recipe, above)
1–2 sweet, ripe peaches, pitted and chopped
Ice to fill blender

Blend on high until fully whipped! A wonderful refresher on a hot day. Try it with pear—it keeps the bowels moving. Any fruit will do here. Try grapes, cherries, berries, kiwis, and more!

SUN TEA

1 cup dried herbs, any variety or combination
¾ gallon charged water

Put charged water in glass gallon jar with a cup of dried herbal tea. Tea can be put into a large tea ball, a large hemp tea bag, or placed in loose and strained after sun and before refrigeration. Place in direct sunshine for a few hours, or on the radiator or over a pilot light, to brew tea. Many teas, especially leaf or flower, will brew with very little sun or heat. When brewed, remember to strain the herbs out, as they will ferment otherwise. Sweeten if you like with honey, maple syrup, or stevia herb, or make a punch by adding a sweet fruit juice.

Makes ¾ gallon.

Favorite combinations

- Good Digestion Tea: peppermint and licorice (whole or ground)
- Youthing Formula: angelica root (ground) and sage
- Night Vision and Good Eyesight Tea: bilberry (ground) and gingko leaf

FLYING TEA

1 cup hibiscus flowers, dried, loosely packed
½ cup rosehip petals, dried ground or whole
Stevia herb, raw honey, or maple syrup, to taste

Make a *Sun Tea* (see recipe, above), using hibiscus flowers and rosehip petals. Sweeten with stevia herb, raw honey, or maple syrup. Dark red pigments in foods are good medicine for radiation exposure. Loaded with anti-oxidant Vitamin C, this tea stops free-radical damage (aging) incurred through traveling by car or airplane, computer work, sunburn, breathing toxic substances, etc. Most live within a sea of electromagnetic energy. Replenish yourself with this beautiful red tea. It's so delicious, kids think it's cherry Kool-Aid.

FRESH GINGER TEA

1 2-inch piece ginger root
4 cups charged water
2 slices of lemon

Chop the ginger root into small pieces, grate it, or press in a ginger press. Add to charged water in a small pot over the stove. Warm to desired temperature, keeping the water well under the boiling point. Pour through a strainer into cups with a slice of lemon.

Serves 2.

Secret Teaching: Ginger has a warming effect on the body. It strongly stimulates the action of digestion and circulation and helps soothe flatulence and colic. Keep the tea warm in a thermos for winter hikes and ski trips. Nice with a cinnamon stick or sprinkle of powdered cinnamon.

HYDRATING WARM MEDICINAL TEA

Herb or herbal combination, usually 1 or 2 heaping teaspoons, or 2
   teabags
12 ounces of charged water

Heat water until it is just under the boiling point. Brew your herbs in a Ball jar with lid for 15 minutes or so. Strain off your tea and add lemon or honey if desired.

This is a good way to start the day. Wondering which herbs to take? I like to vary my herbs. My favorite boxed tea is Raja's Cup for its amazing ability to stop free-radical damage and its rich flavorful taste, though I tend to go for loose tea and I choose herbs for their medicinal qualities. Choose herbal teas rather than black teas.

Everyone should have a good herbal book on hand to dose the symptoms that come and go in everyday life. Whole herbs are very safe, especially when taken as a tea. Some herbs have gotten a bad rap lately, such as gingko, because the whole herbs were tinkered with in a lab and sold in pills as an extract. The most desirable properties in these plants were isolated and potentiated. Other aspects of the plant were removed. Even in this way herbs are relatively harmless and only in rare cases is there a challenge, especially when compared to pharmaceutical grade drugs and their myriad of side effects. This is avoided by using the whole herb, decanted as a tea.

WARM GINGER CIDER

    4 cups fresh raw apple cider
    Sprinkle of cinnamon powder, or ½ cinnamon stick
    Slices of orange or lemon
    Fresh ground ginger root
    1 tablespoon cloves, whole

Mix all ingredients together in a saucepan over the stove and warm. Strain into cups. This cider has a rich aroma that fills the home.

    Serves 2.

PRUNE JUICE

    10–15 organic prunes, pitted
    2–3 cups charged water

Soak prunes overnight in charged water. Put prunes and soak water in blender and blend 2 minutes until liquefied. This will get the bowels moving in the morning—a safe laxative.

FRIENDLY FERMENTS

REJUVELAC
    2 cups soft white wheat berries, or kamut
    1 gallon charged water
    2 capsules acidophilus, any kind (optional though encouraged)

Soak grain overnight and sprout 2 days. Blend half the grain with charged water in a blender. Pulse a few seconds only, just to break the grain, rather than to liquefy. Place in a glass gallon jar. Blend the second half of the grains, as above, and add to jar. Empty acidophilus capsules, and discard empty capsule. Stir.

FERMENTING: Cover mouth of jar with a breathable cloth, like a thin cotton towel, and secure with a rubber band. Place the jar in a warm place, such as the top of the refrigerator (out of direct sunlight) for 2 days. The ideal temperature is between 75–80°F. Often the cupboard above the refrigerator is warm and an ideal place to ferment. If the place you choose isn't dark, simply cover jar with a towel. It will take a day or two longer to ferment if the temperature varies much.

Ferment for 2 days. Pour the water into a gallon jar, straining the grains out. This is your first batch of Rejuvelac. Store sealed in the refrigerator. It keeps for a week or so. You can make a second and third batch by reusing the grain. Cover the grain in the jar with charged water to fill the gallon container ⅔ full. Add more acidophilus and give it a stir. The second and third batches take only one day each to ferment. After 24 hours, strain grains off as above. Drink as a refreshing beverage and use in place of water in recipes. Rejuvelac adds nutrition and zing to any sauce. Make a tasty drink by mixing with fruit juice. We all need more ferments. Adding acidophilus guarantees a certain strain of bacteria will grow. It prevents stinky-sock tasting *Rejuvelac.*

Secret Teaching: Ferments, like Rejuvelac *and* Cabbage Lemon Elixir *(see recipe, below) are excellent sources of friendly bacteria. Anyone who was not breast-fed, has had a life of cooked and starchy carbohydrates, antibiotic pharmaceuticals, or suffers from run-away yeast conditions, like candida, desperately requires friendly bacteria. Even flying in airplanes reduces our friendly bacteria count, which is why most people feel constipated after they fly. Dose up on friendly ferments like* Rejuvelac *and sauerkraut before and after you fly so you're always feeling good. These recipes contain many millions of helpful bacteria that crowd out unfriendly, opportunistic bacteria. The helpful bacteria found here is much more potent and viable then any store-bought liquid or dry capsule bacteria, though they are helpful. Babies do well with* Rejuvelac.

NOTE: Rejuvelac *can be used for douching and enemas. Always dilute with charged water. One cup* Rejuvelac *to 8 cups charged water can be very helpful in bringing the vaginal canal and intestine pH back into balance.*

CABBAGE LEMON ELIXIR

Small organic cabbage, cored and chopped
Whole lemon, yellow skin removed, white pith intact
Charged water

Fill blender ⅓ with cabbage. Add half the lemon and charged water to half-full in the blender. Pulse to blend, rather than liquefy. Transfer to glass gallon jar. Repeat process with remaining cabbage. Fill jar to almost full with charged water. Put in a warm place (like *Rejuvelac*) for 24–36 hours depending on temperature; more heat equals less time. Pour the Elixir into a gallon jar and strain out cabbage. Store in the refrigerator.

Makes 1 batch.

Secret Teaching: Ferments, like this elixir, are good for healing skin, lungs, and digestive tract. Ferments are important in recolonizing the colon with proper bacteria (biffido bacterium) that live in the large intestine. Ferments create the right pH in the colon. See more in pH (Parts of Hydrogen), *p. 252.*

KOMBUCHA (MUSHROOM) TEA

1 "baby" Kombucha mushroom
12 cups charged water
1 handful black tea, ground to a fine powder
1 cup raw sugar

1 cup raw honey, to use on your third batch with the same
  mushroom

Remove all rings off your fingers before handling mushrooms and always keep metal away from Kombucha mushrooms.

Obtain a "baby" Kombucha mushroom from someone who grows them or makes Kombucha tea regularly, or order one from your health food store. A new "baby" mushroom comes from each batch you make. Combine water and tea in a glass container and place in the sun for the day to brew.

Strain out the tea grounds and put tea into glass gallon jar with a relatively large mouth so you can easily remove the mushroom after tea is made. (The mushroom will grow to the size of the container it is grown in.) Add raw sugar to tea. Stir well. Add your "baby" mushroom. Place a cotton cloth over the entire jar and a rubber band over the mouth of the jar to keep cloth in place and to allow the tea to breathe. It is best kept at room temperature. Leave it there for 6–7 days.

Remember to remove your finger rings, and then remove the mushroom and the new "baby" that will have grown underneath it. Carefully separate the original mushroom from the new one. Every third batch can be made with 1 cup of raw honey alone. This makes the most delicate champagne-like brew! Simply make this batch with water and honey only. The mushroom must have been used to make the first 2 batches consecutively for it to be used in this way.

Store in refrigerator, covered. Drink 4 ounces in the morning on an empty stomach for best results and 4 ounces at night. It is recommended to drink 8 ounces or less per day. Adding 10–15 raisins to your Kombucha sweetens it pleasantly.

Start a new batch with one mushroom and gift your new "baby" to a friend. Both the "mother"" and the "baby" will continue to produce batches of tea. Each new batch will produce a new "baby" to gift away and make more batches. They store well covered in the refrigerator while you find new homes for them.

HOT SHOTZ

  2 lemons, yellow skin removed, white pith intact
  1 1½-inch piece ginger root
  1 hot pepper, or ¼ teaspoon cayenne powder, mild or hot
  2 cups charged water

Chop the lemons and put into blender. Peel ginger and likewise chop and place in blender with your preferred hot pepper (jalapeño or another favorite pepper). Blend well. This is a great way to start the day. Drink 2 ounces first thing in the morning to really clear the throat and get the blood moving. Keep remainder, covered in the refrigerator. For those with sensitive teeth, try using a straw to pass the lemon by the dentin of the teeth.

WATERMELON WHIP

  1 watermelon
  Charged water

Slice watermelon and cut the rind off and discard it. Cut watermelon into chunks and remove seeds. Fill the blender with watermelon chunks and pour in charged water to fill. With a wooden spoon crush the melon well so it will blend. Blend on high 30 seconds until frothy. Serve in tall glasses—delicious and pretty.

Secret Teaching: Watermelon has natural refrigerant properties and is cooling to the body on hot summer days. Choose fertile foods with seeds rather than sterile seedless varieties.

FRUIT PUNCH

   1 medium ripe pineapple, peeled, cored, and cut into chunks

   3 oranges, peeled

   2 limes, peeled

   3 lemons, yellow skin removed, white pith intact

   Honey, stevia herb, or maple syrup, to sweeten

   12 cups charged water

Juice pineapple, oranges, and limes and put them into gallon glass container. In a blender add lemons, honey, and charged water. Blend on medium, then high until whipped. Pour into the gallon glass container. Give it a stir. Adjust sweetener to taste. Store sealed in the refrigerator. Will keep for several days. Kids love it!

ANNIE'S FAVORITE GREEN DRINK

   2 cucumbers, or ½ bunch celery

   2 hard Granny Smith apples

   1 head kale, about 7 leaves

   1 lemon, yellow skin removed, white pith intact

Juice everything and enjoy immediately. This is a real refresher that cleans up the blood instantly and gives you more brain power with the extra greens. Substitute any greens for kale. I like kale because any juicer can juice it, whereas most juicers have trouble juicing leafy greens.

PYCNOGENOL "WINE"

Several large bunches of grapes, with seeds, such as: concord, black,
or red

Pluck grapes from stems and wash. If you are freezing them, place in a
Ziploc bag and freeze several hours or longer. Otherwise keep them on
the stems until you are ready to use them (this keeps them fresher).
Run grapes, either frozen, chilled, or room temperature, through your
juicer for an incredible grape *faux* wine. Very nice when served in gob-
lets with dinner. Or, instead of juicing, use a blender and blend very
well, about 2 minutes, to thoroughly liquefy seeds to an assimilable
form. If your blender lacks the force to blend the seeds down to nothing, you may need to strain before serving.

Makes 1 tall glass or 2 wine glasses.

*Secret Teaching: Grape seeds contain powerful anti-oxidants that are special
and unique. They contain bioflavonoids, called pycnogenols. These anti-
oxidants are 20% stronger than vitamin C and 50% stronger than vitamin E! This is a great beverage to refresh yourself during long hours of
working on the computer, or to take along in the car or airplane to combat the free-radical effects of radiation. Cell damage due to free radicals is at the root of most health challenges; it is the process of aging.*

PYCNOGENOL PASSION

1 cascade of grapes with seeds (like black grapes)
1 cup black cherries, pitted and frozen
½ cup manuka, or other seeded raisin, soaked 1 hour in ½ cup
    charged water, soak water reserved
½ ripe avocado
2 cup unpasteurized juice (like apple or orange)
2 tablespoons flax seed oil

Pluck grapes from stem and freeze in a Ziploc bag, or use at room temperature. Blend all ingredients together in blender until smooth, about 2 full minutes depending on how powerful your blender is. Make sure the seeds are completely ground. Spoon into sorbet glasses and garnish. Read the Secret Teaching on the healing power of Pycnogenols (above).

ALMOND MILK

1 cup raw almonds, soaked 4 or more hours
3–6 cups charged water
3 tablespoons raw honey or maple syrup, or 1 tablespoon stevia herb
Pinch of Celtic sea salt

Blend all ingredients in blender until creamy and smooth. If you like it thinner, add more water and strain. If you prefer it thicker, add less water and you'll have a thick "whipped cream" consistency to spoon onto fruit meals, such as *Essene French Toast* (see recipe, p. 182). Nut milk is great on *Muesli Buckwheaties* (see recipe, p. 183). Store capped in the refrigerator. Keeps for several days. Use in place of dairy milk for all purposes. Makes a delicious milk.

BRAZIL NUT MILK

1 cup raw Brazil nuts, soaked in charged water to cover

6 cups charged water

1–3 tablespoons honey, or more to taste

¼ teaspoon salt

1 tablespoons lecithin granules

2 tablespoons coconut butter

1 tablespoon vanilla extract (non-alcohol)

Pre-soak Brazil nuts for 15 minutes. Drain them, rinse well, and discard soak water. Add fresh charged water—more for a milk consistency, less for a thicker crème. Blend all ingredients until smooth, about 2 minutes. Strain well through a fine-meshed stainless steel strainer, or an organic cloth-straining bag. Strain it twice for milk that doesn't separate. Keeps well refrigerated, sealed in bottles. Use in place of dairy milk. Delicious heated for a Chai Latte.

SUNFLOWER SESAME MILK

½ cup sunflower seeds, soaked 1 hour, drained and rinsed

½ cup sesame seeds, ground to a meal

3 cups charged water

1 tablespoon lecithin granules

2 tablespoons honey, or 1 tablespoon liquid stevia herb

¼ teaspoon Celtic sea salt

Soak sunflower seeds for 1 hour, then drain and rinse. Grind sesame seeds in a coffee grinder. Combine all ingredients in a blender and blend well on high for several minutes, until liquefied. Strain if desired. Seed and nut milk replace dairy on a transition diet from animal protein to LifeFood. Experiment with different nuts and seeds to create your own delicious milks.

PHAT MIDNIGHT MILK

½ cup black sesame seeds
½ cup un-hulled sesame seeds
3 cups charged water
3 tablespoons honey or maple syrup, or 10 seeded raisins, soaked in
   charged water to cover, soak water reserved
¼ teaspoon Celtic sea salt

Grind both sesame seeds to a moist meal in a coffee grinder. Blend with charged water and sweeten with maple syrup, honey, or soaked raisins with their soak water. For thinner milk, just add more soak water (about ⅔ cup water). This is a high-calcium bone-building drink.

MACADAMIA NUT MILK

5 cups charged water
1 cup raw macadamia nuts
1 tablespoon lecithin granules
1 tablespoon raw honey or maple syrup (optional)
¼ teaspoon Celtic sea salt

Put all ingredients into blender carafe and let sit with lid on for 10 minutes to soften the nuts. Blend well on high speed for up 1 minute.

This is a rich and yummy milk. Always have a nut or seed milk made up in your refrigerator. It really satisfies by itself as a beverage, and can also easily let you create a quick snack or light meal by pouring milk over *Muesli Buckwheaties* (see recipe, p. 183), over a bowl of berries, or with almonds, raisins, and shredded coconut. Make this recipe with less water to create a nut crème. Layered with fruit, this type of sweet crème makes a stunning dessert.

CAROB MINT MILK

2 cups any nut milk or seed milk (see recipes, above)

2 tablespoons raw carob powder, or more to taste

2 tablespoons raw honey, or maple syrup, or 1 tablespoon liquid
stevia herb

2 drops peppermint essential oil, or 1 tablespoon dried peppermint

Blend in Vita-Mix 30 seconds, or 2 minutes in a regular blender. A yummy sweet protein treat. Helps children break packaged soymilk addictions. Try a fun variation by blending with ice cubes and making a milkshake.

RASPBERRY SUNFLOWER MILKSHAKE

Pycnogenol (anti-oxidant) Power!

1 cup raspberries, or any berries, frozen

1 cup seeded grapes (like concord, black, red, etc.)

1 cup sunflower seeds

Pinch Celtic sea salt

2 tablespoons raw honey or maple syrup (optional)

½ teaspoon vanilla extract (optional)

5–6 ice cubes (made from charged water)

Soak sunflower seeds in water for about 20 minutes, drain, rinse, and discard water. Blend all ingredients in blender well until both berry seeds and grape seeds are thoroughly blended.

A meal for 2, or a snack for 4.

CHAPTER 8

SAMPLE MENUS

A lovely table includes complementary colors to stimulate the eye as well as the appetite. For example, if my table had only two colors, say green and brown, I would slice a plate of tomato, and add basil and Celtic sea salt. Perhaps I'd shred some butternut squash and sweeten it with apple juice and a few raisins, thus adding the colors red and orange to the spread. This elegant maneuver would probably cost under 2 dollars and would activate the salivary glands of everyone present.

For many newcomers the challenge is to present a balance of flavors that combine well and are easy to digest. Always taste the produce before preparation, as you'll find that fresh seasonal fruits and vegetables will hardly need any seasoning at all. Whereas out of season or hothouse-grown produce may require a sauce or dressing to enhance its features. It's a good idea to eat with chopsticks whenever possible as this slows down the speed of shoveling and invites the eater to chew the food more thoroughly, to a liquid.

WHAT'S FOR BREAKFAST?

Good Day Starters

Hot Shotz, 2 ounces	recipe, p. 194
Hydrating Warm Medicinal Tea, 12 ounces	recipe, p. 189
Carob Mint Milk (or other nut milk)	recipe, p. 200
Raw Fruit, or Vegetable, Juice with ground Flax seed	

Heartier Fare

• Muesli Buckwheaties	recipe, p. 183
with Almond Milk and Fresh Blueberries	
• Smoothie	recipe, pp. 158–163
• Fresh Seasonal Fruit	
• Papaya with a Squeeze of Fresh Lime	
• Fruit Salad with Cinnamon Raisin Sauce	
• Fruit Bowl with Orange Fig Frosting	frosting, p. 173
• Phat Black Sorbet	recipe, p. 166
• Creamy Mango Sorbet	recipe, p. 168
with Carob Syrup and Chopped Almonds	
• Essene French Toast	recipe, p. 183
with	
• Vanilla Maple Crème	recipe, p. 147
and Blueberries and Raisins	

Very Low Glycemic Index

• Avocado Half Drizzled with Oil	
• 10 olives and handful of nuts or seeds	
• Any Soup	see Chapter 1, p. 59
• Cherry Nut Milk Smoothie	recipe, p. 159
• Carob Mint Milk	recipe, p. 200

WHAT'S FOR LUNCH & DINNER?

The ideal LifeFood meal begins with a fresh raw juice for an appetizer, or aperitif, if you will. We make a juice, relax while we drink it, and then begin preparations for our meal. All city-dwellers and road-travelers breathe exhaust fumes and can greatly benefit from a dark green vegetable juice combo like apple, cucumber, and kale! It's a personal favorite that we have nearly every day we are in a city. Vegetables and particularly dark leafy greens help us cart out heavy metals from the bloodstream. Can't get enough of that dark green stuff!

Remember to always chew what you drink and drink what you chew. Chewing is very important because a hormone, parotoid, is released in saliva that nourishes every single cell of your body. Chewing stimulates the digestive juices in the mouth and gets starch-splitting enzymes active. so digestion begins as food enters the upper enzymatic stomach.

Example #1
Raven's Electric Moss
Avocado half w/scoop sauerkraut
10–15 raw macadamia nuts
Garden Salad

Example #2
Juicy Cucumber Soup
Humus on Essene Crackers

Example #3
Miso Soup
Oil & Garlic "Pasta"
Bowl of dried dulse

Example #4
The "DLT"
Dark Leafy Greens with Tahini Tamari Dressing
Mexican Cucumbers

Example #5
Super Sandwiches
Bugs On A Log
Coleslaw

Example #6
Coconut Orgasm Soup
Guacamole
Hot Sauce and Flax Crackers

Example #7
Nori Rolls
Oriental Sesame Marinated Zucchini
Sea Liscious Snacks

Example #8
Zucchini "Pasta" with Pesto Sauce
*SEA*sar Salad

Example #9
Seventh Heaven Soup
Nutty Lentil Salad
Sun Rich Yams

Example #10
Greek Salad
Spicy Pumpkin Seeds
Tabouli

Example #11
Spicy Ginger Tofu
Dark Leafy Greens with Lemon Ginger Vinaigrette
Poppy seed Crackers

CHAPTER 9

LOTIONS, POTIONS, & TINCTURES

Herbs are the highest vibe plants around. They seem to possess an inherent wisdom that is only like unto itself. Herbs are an important component of the LifeFood diet. They are most often wild crafted, picked as they grow in the wild. And, as such, they have had to fight off mold, fungus, bacteria, parasites, and vermin to survive. They possess a much higher life force frequency and have many more minerals and a broad range of trace elements and vitamins that are unusual in their high levels and bioavailability.

LONGEVITY TONIC

1 part ginseng root
1 part dong quai
1 part ginkgo
½ part gota kola
½ part fo-ti

Obtain herbs in their whole dried form and grind them yourself in your Vita-mix or grain/coffee grinder. Roots like ginseng can be grated by hand first with a hand grater. Grind to a powder and mix all ingredients together well. Place in a tightly capped glass jar. We store ours in the refrigerator to keep fresh.

Use 1–2 heaping teaspoons per day. Either mix it with a little raw fresh juice or eat it with plenty of saliva to chew it with and chew it well. It makes a nice medicinal tea when added to 12 ounces of hot water and brewed for 15 minutes in a Ball jar with the lid tightly sealed. Strain and drink hot. It is an acquired taste that you will grow to love. Keep it in your mouth for as long as possible as the membranes under the tongue are the thinnest in the body for rapid uptake to the brain.

These are longevity, vitality, and mental alertness herbs that have been used for thousands of years. Use them every day for 3–4 months, and then relax on them for the rest of the year using only 3 or 4 tablespoons per week. It is generally recommended for pregnant women to choose to skip ginseng as it contains a naturally occurring steroid. Children can take half the dosage of an adult, according to size. Renewed vitality can be achieved through the regular use of this blend! I personally attribute it to my sudden ¾-inch growth-spurt, in height, during one 4-month program!!

Ginkgo has flavanoids that are involved in a number of functions, including the manufacture of prostocyclin. Prostocyclin is produced by the endothelial cells lining the passageways of the blood vessels. Prostocyclin allows blood cells to slip frictionless through these blood vessels. Two days after ingestion, ginkgo is found in three major places in the body: the hippocampus (long-term memory), the eyes, and in the adrenals.

Ginseng has adaptogenic properties that strengthen the body to help handle both physical and psychological stress. Ginseng is known for its longevity effects. It contains saponins that lower surface tension and help the body form emulsions from cholesterol to manufacture hormones. These saponins alter cell wall permeability, enhancing the cell's ability to absorb nutrients.

ANTIFUNGAL TREATMENT

1 teaspoon pau d'arco
1 teaspoon chaparral
1 teaspoon golden seal herb
2 tablespoons DMSO
1 teaspoon vitamin E oil
½ teaspoon tea tree oil
Charged water

This is great for athlete's foot. Obtain the pau d'arco, chaparral, and golden seal herb in the powdered form, or grind it yourself. Mix all ingredients into a stiff paste, adding drops of charged water if needed. Store in a tightly sealed glass container in the refrigerator.

Use this combination to wipe out stubborn long-term athlete's foot by smearing enough paste to cover affected area, especially between toes. Put on a clean pair of natural fiber socks and relax. The socks may become stained from the golden seal. Allow it to dry completely. This can be done twice or more daily for instant relief. Continue until symptoms clear and then for 2 more days to completely snuff out the fungus.

Remember that this is just to fix the symptom of fungus. Fungus arises out of filth in the body. It can only grow where there is a rich growing ground for mold, fungus, and yeast. Eliminate starches, do a LifeFood Nutritional Fast, and eat LifeFood, and you'll be healing the issue at its root.

TOPICAL FUNGAL TREATMENT

2 capsules broad-spectrum enzyme, Hi-Zymes brand, or another
    brand
1 capsule vitamin C
1 capsule L-Lysine
1 teaspoon pau d'arco herb, powdered
2 teaspoons DMSO
¼ teaspoon golden seal herb
10 drops liquid vitamin E
Few drops charged or distilled water

Empty capsules, or powder pressed-pills in a grinder. Mix all ingredients in a small bowl until it's the consistency of a stiff paste, adding drops of charged water to be creamy enough to stick to the skin. Store in a tightly capped glass container in the refrigerator.

Apply to affected area 2 or 3 times daily for best results. Let it air dry for a while. Keep affected area moistened with the paste. Remarkably the inflammation will usually subside within an hour or so. Used at the first signs of outbreak this will often dissuade it. Keep the paste on as long as possible and put some on before bedtime. Be aware that the golden seal will stain things bright yellow.

As always when using DMSO, keep all BandAids, plastic, make-up, lotions, dyes, artificial ingredients, petrol chemicals, sunscreens, etc. away from skin and DMSO.

DMSO

DMSO (dimethyl sulfoxide), at 99.9% purity, is nature's wonderful healer. It is a by-product of the paper industry and is therefore in abundance. DMSO is a muscle relaxer, a natural anaesthetic, and is often used for relief from burns, sprains, and inflammation, and it's a solvent. Sperm is stored in DMSO in sperm banks to keep the sperm cell structure in tact during its frozen state.

We use DMSO in topical herbal applications to carry the medicinal elements to the bone where it can do the most good. When using DMSO be very careful to apply it only to skin that is completely free of toxins (i.e., soap, perfume, lotions, petrochemicals, dyes, make-up, and all artificial ingredients), as the DMSO will carry what it touches into the body and down to the bone.

DMSO can bring great relief to sore muscles, sprains, burns, and inflammation by diluting and rubbing into the skin. Dilute DMSO with 30% charged water as the DMSO has a heating element to it. It will heat up (exothermic reaction). A dilution of no more than 50% below the waist and no more than 30% above the waist; culminating in no more than 1% for the eyes. Dilute it more the closer it is used toward the head. Chemicals and other exogenous toxins can cause free-radical damage. When this occurs to the water molecules that compose our bodies, hydroxyl radicals are created. DMSO binds with these hydroxyl radicals making them inert so the body can naturally filter them out (urinate) through the kidneys.

In all less than vita conditions, hydroxyl radicals are formed. Thus DMSO may be indicated to help the body heal itself. DMSO has antiparasitic properties and helps change cell membrane permeability in order that cell respiration and restoration is enhanced. It tends to cause a build-up of white blood cells and increases macrophage (large white blood cells) migration. Because DMSO has the remarkable property of substituting water in a cell it can help restore cell integrity by neutralizing free radicals within the cell. Combined with vitamin E it can act as a solvent for restoring the collegian in scar tissue.

MENSTRUAL SPONGE

For women in the know. Completely natural! Dioxin-free! Bio-friendly!

1 sea sponge, all-natural, no dyes or coloring

Cut sea sponge into a tampon shape, about twice the size of a tampon, as sponge reduces when wet. Wet your sponge with water, squeezing out the excess, and insert as you would an applicator-free tampon. The sponge is quite easy to shape and you can push it in with your finger to a comfortable position. It is very comfortable.

Rinse your sponge every few hours, and very well before bedtime, by running water over it and squeezing it until it is clean and smells fresh. Of course, as you eat 85%–90% LifeFood, your menstrual flow will gradually decrease as the body optimizes itself.

The menstrual sponge completely eliminates the waste (trees!), pollution (landfills!), and risk (toxic shock syndrome!) of commercially made tampons or pads. Most tampons and pads are bleached white with the most deadly of toxins: dioxin. This is one of the most powerful toxins known to man. It is measured in parts per billion, and the smallest amount can shock the whole system. Anything inserted into the vagina should be all-natural and completely organic. Bleached products should be completely eliminated.

At the end of your cycle simply cleanse the sponge by putting it in about 2 cups charged water with 2 tablespoons hydrogen peroxide (food grade if you can find it) for about 24 hours. Then air dry your sponge and store it for your next moon. Anytime the sponge smells a little funky simply wash it with an all-natural shampoo (no SLS) and rinse well. These sponges are very affordable and biodegradable, so I just flush mine down the toilet when I'm done with it, and use a new one next moon.

ANTIPERSPIRANT & BREAST HEALTH

Today many women shave their underarms and then within minutes apply an antiperspirant. I have stood for an hour at supermarkets everywhere looking at antiperspirant labels, and just about every one lists aluminum as the active ingredient. Aluminum is a manmade metal that spins in the opposite direction of organic material. It is believed to be toxic to the body and is found in abundance in the brain tissue of Alzheimer patients. So, back to shaving and antiperspirant, here you have the skin pores being opened in the act of shaving the underarm, and a product containing aluminum and who knows what else directly applied. This material then has a portal entry into the body, very near the lymph gland and the breast.

It is my sneaking suspicion that this is a contributing factor in today's tremendous rise in breast cancer. Daily use of underwire bras can also be a factor. Use one of the natural deodorants found in your health food store. Shave your underarms at night rather than the morning. And remember, the skin is the largest organ of elimination and the whole body perspires.

SECRET DAKINI AFTER-BATH BODY OIL

 3 tablespoons DMSO at 99.9% purity
1 cup jojoba oil, or a mix of pure slow- and cold-pressed organic oils
¼ cup castor oil
20 drops high-quality amber Vitamin E oil
5 drops each: lavender and rose essential oil, or other mixed oils

Combine all ingredients in a very hard plastic bottle that has a squirt cap. Give it a good shake before using. After bath, and while glistening wet, massage oil into every part of your body. Massage it in to your face, neck, and shoulders and work your way down to the toes. Have a friend rub it into the skin on your back. Spend extra time and oil on sunburn, or any skin needing extra care. Make a larger batch and store in a dark, cool place, preferably in the refrigerator. Store in glass for the long term.

When bathing use only all-natural organic products. Avoid the dreaded sodium laurel sulphate (SLS). It is a foaming agent that everyone can avoid. Yet, it's everywhere. Demand SLS-free products at your health food store. Do you have a shower filter on your shower yet? Get one that filters out chlorine and other toxins regularly found in tap water.

GINGER STEAM FACIAL

 2 tablespoons (approximately) fresh ginger root, grated
12–20 ounces charged water,

This clears the lungs and makes the skin fresh and clear. Place grated ginger into a large bowl, and have a big bath towel nearby. Heat the water to a boil, and then pour over ginger into the bowl. Bring your face to the steam and inhale, gently at first. Cover your head with the towel and breathe the ginger steam deeply into your lungs. After 10 minutes, splash cold water onto your face and enjoy a cool glass of charged water.

AVOCADO MASK

Mash 2 tablespoons fresh ripe avocado very well with a fork. A little goes a long way. Spread thinly over clean face, neck, and the back of the hands. Leave on until it dries, about 10 minutes, and then rinse off with warm water or a wet, hot washcloth. The skin feels fresh and taut and soft as can be. Great after the *Ginger Steam Facial.*

Exfoliation Variation: Grind up 1 tablespoon steel-cut rolled oats and mix into mashed avocado to add a deep-cleansing scrubbing action to the mask. Massage it on well and let dry, then rinse off.

CUCUMBER FACIAL

Take the cucumber rind from your peeled cucumber and rub all over face and neck. It cools the skin and freshens up the pores, acting as a natural astringent. Cucumber pulp will take the sting out of a burn. Refresh tired eyes by placing cucumber slices over eyelids and relaxing for 10 minutes, or during a scented bath.

CARROT MASK

Take carrot pulp from juicing and mix with honey and avocado and a little charged water, to bind. Make a mask and rest 20 minutes in the tub or sofa, rinse. A great use for carrots!

CHAPTER 10

LIFEFOOD NUTRITIONAL FASTING

By resting the digestive system of the body one can attain purity of the body, speech, and mind. We overwork the digestion more often than not. Rarely do I see a truly healthy person. When I am bored in a public place, I play the "spot the healthy person" game. Most everyone is digestively exhausted. This is the cause of all disease. By resting the digestive tract and eliminating bile stones in the bile bladder, thereby relieving the pressure in the abdominal cavity, true health can be obtained. A system that has sluggish septic or garbage disposal is a sick unit indeed. This is the root of all illness.

THE LIFEFOOD NUTRITIONAL FAST

LifeFood Nutritional Fasting consists of consuming juiced and blended food. Fasting on blended and juiced foods gives the digestive system a rest. Most Americans are digestively exhausted and this type of a diet for a 14-day period, is recommended several times a year. The person recovering from illness can even stay on the blended foods for months, until symptoms subside. With blended food, especially LifeFood soup, the person is often getting more nutrition than in entire meals of cooked and processed food.

Juicing is a great way to stock up on many whole vitamins and minerals. Remember to chew your juice because chewing stimulates the secretion of digestive enzymes in the mouth and stomach. Juicing provides excellent nutrition while affording the body a rest from digestion. The fiber in juice is broken down, saving the body from having to break it down. Most people swallow large pieces of whole foods and expect the stomach to just break it down. For sugar sensitive people, 2 or 3 tablespoons of ground flax seed can be added to any juice or soup, or over any food for that matter. Ground flax seeds (fat and protein) aid in balancing sugar released into the bloodstream so the person is more comfortable.

The downside to juicing is that it masticates the cell wall of the whole food. Blending is preferable, as it retains all the fiber and goodness of the food. Juicing removes the fiber and can create an unnatural access to fast-moving sugar. We love to have blended meals, fast 1 or 2 days each week, and do several 14-day fasts a year. During these fasts we usually have very good energy and often exercise with a light jog each day and plenty of rest.

A urine analysis of the fasting person can reveal up to 200 times the amount of toxins as a non-fasting person. Where did these toxins come from? They were stored in every conceivable place in the body until a time, when the body is fasting, that it can begin to clean house. Fasting is an essential practice for longevity. All animals in the wild will fast if they aren't feeling well. They seek out medicinal herbs and fast on these and pure water. Animals in the wild usually die of old age, while domesticated animals (fed dead canned and dry food) now mimic our human capacity for disease.

Most folks eat at least 3 meals a day of low-amplitude food, which keeps their body always digesting this material. Imagine the body as a huge factory with thousands of busy workers conducting the business of the body. Day and night they process, digest, or store because they cannot assimilate these non-nutrients. Now begin a fast and give these workers free time to take the week off and they will take the opportunity to start to clean and buff the factory and cart away waste material.

It is common at our juice fast training, The Purification Journey, for a person to have a large bowel movement on the third day of the fast and feel great relief. This is largely due to low counts of friendly bacteria and a sluggish intestinal tract. It is beneficial to rejuvenate the body periodically through fasting. Many symptoms and conditions improve, clear up, or go into remission through fasting. Many times we've witnessed tumors shrink and disappear through LifeFood Nutritional Fasting. Removing starch from the diet is essential for healing chronic illness.

When doing a simple 7-day fast, here's what to expect. Day 1 and 2 you can expect knee-jerk responses that you have to eat—i.e., mealtimes, the smells of food, the social aspect of meals. Day 3 is usually a breeze as you've released much of the material in the bowel. This creates a great freedom in the brain; you become more coherent. The response-to-fast is stronger than the response-to-eat at this point as well. Days 4, 5, and 6 are very etheric, and a calm spiritual climate shapes your environment. Day 7 is a slow re-entry to food, usually a smoothie or LifeFood blended soup. Toward the end of the day you might have a fruit meal. It is generally recommended to continue a fast until the desire to eat returns.

All creatures operate more effectively on a light or empty stomach. Whenever we have to be really "on," we like to fast to prepare and just take in nutritional beverages like soup, juice, Rejuvelac, nut and seed milk. Add a fresh raw juice to your day.

City-dwellers, and everyone, can benefit from a fresh, raw vegetable juice with dark, leafy greens. Juices like apple, cucumber, and kale are real tonics. Dark leafy greens help us transmutate high levels of carbon monoxide (exhaust) in the environment. Vegetables, unlike fruit, help us cart out heavy metals from the bloodstream. Fruitarian diets (eating only fruit) are most effective in clean-air environments with plenty of clean water for drinking and bathing, and with a nice amount of sunshine.

CLEANSING REACTIONS

We mentioned that the fasting person could have up to 200 times the amount of toxins in their urine than the non-fasting person. During a fast, or even just switching from a dead food diet to a LifeFood diet, the body will dump toxins from fat cells into the blood, melt plaque along veins and arteries, secrete bile from the liver, and activate many other detox pathways to refresh and regenerate the body. What effects can be expected from this activity? A cleansing reaction occurs. Cleansing reactions can range from mucus and phlegm rising to the surface, as in a runny nose, cough, low energy, nausea, headache, mood swings, dizziness, or a mild fever or chill. Most of these symptoms are as a result of a sluggish colon and a sign to take more laxatives and keep the LifeFood beverages and soups up. Stay hydrated.

These are all *positive* signs that the body is unloading its carefully stashed supply of dietary and environmental toxins. Let them go! People in relatively good health can continue to fast through these cleansing reactions. Very frail people will want to slow the cleanse by adding lots of ground flax seeds to what they consume. Whole cooked food will stop a cleanse, often entirely. The purpose of fasting is to detoxify at a rate tolerable for the individual person.

THE 14-DAY LIFEFOOD NUTRITIONAL FAST

4 THINGS TO AVOID

SOLID FOOD—Consume raw blended beverages

STARCH—Omit grain, carrot, beets, corn, dates, etc. (See *Starch, Hybrids, and Runaway Sugar,* p. 19.)

ANIMAL FLESH FOOD, DAIRY, & EGGS

COOKED FOOD—including pasteurized juices

WHAT TO HAVE

Organic Seasonal LifeFood Beverages and Soups:

Soup (blended well to a smooth consistency)

Green Drink

Nut and Seed Milk (Brazil Nut Milk)

Smoothies

Sorbet

Raw Juices (unpasteurized), especially vegetable juice

Electrolyte Lemonade

Blended Fruit with Coconut Water

Rejuvelac, or Cabbage Lemon Elixir

Medicinal Herbal Sun Tea (Flying Tea)

Charged Water (Trinity and Evian brands are good)

Add Ground Seeds to Beverages or Soups

Grind flax, pumpkin, or sesame seed to a fine meal and stir into your LifeFood beverage (especially fruit beverages) to stabilize blood sugar while removing bile and helping to move through sludge in the intestinal tract.

Add Super Nutrition to Smoothies or Soups

- Spirulina
- Herbs: Ginseng, Angelica, etc.
- Enzymes
- Whole-food Vitamin/Mineral Supplements
- Bee Pollen
- Goat's Whey, or Colostrum
- Aloe Vera
- Flax, Hemp, Borage, Pumpkinseed Oil
- Ginger Root
- Cayenne
- Garlic
- Raw Honey
- Soaked Prunes
- TOCOtreinals (see *Supplements*)

Keep in mind that during this program the body will experience a cleansing process and de-bulking will occur. Drink plenty of fluids, like pure charged alkaline water to stay hydrated.

We always recommend the organs above the diaphragm be cleared first for upstream cleaning. This can be accomplished by performing 3 flushes (see below) within this 14-day program. Once the stones are flushed out, we suggest a 7-day intestinal cleanse, followed by a parasite flush.

STARTING & BREAKING THE FAST

Being kind and gentle is the inner standing that I, and I alone, am responsible for making sure that I use this information in educating myself how to make decisions in the care of my overall health. I understand that nature is the healer within. This means using personal discretion during the fast to manage cleansing. It's better to be cautious, and to have a motto of "less is more." Always stay hydrated and make sure you are having 3–5 bowel movements a day. Any headache or weakness means there is material in the colon that is just sitting there. Take more laxatives (oxy-mag, Swiss Kriss, or pear or prune juice). With enough bowel movements there should be little to no unpleasant cleansing reactions.

BEGIN AND END FAST WITH A BULKING MEAL

To start and break a fast, your final solid food should be a large bulky salad if you're in good health; otherwise, lightly steamed vegetables with a LifeFood sauce are ideal. It should be eaten until you are three-quarters full. The last and first solid food should be thought of as soluble and insoluble fiber. If cooked, it is only mildly nutritive, yet a good broom for beginning the cleanse. These two meals are the broom that sweeps the intestine before and after your fast. It is good to begin and end with a bulking broom-like meal.

Those who do well with sugar may choose to break the fast with fruit; however, a big hearty crunchy salad is a better choice. To be safe, for the average American, go with lightly steamed vegetables prepared with a LifeFood sauce. Always be kind, gentle, and allowing.

STIMULATE 3–5 BOWEL MOVEMENTS A DAY

Make sure the digestive tract and alimentary canal are kept open and moving during any fast. This means you should have 3–5 bowel movements a day. If you consume 3 meals a day then it's good to have 3 bowel movements a day. Most people are intensely constipated. What goes in should come out in a timely manner. Leftover food in a sluggish intestine drains vitality and energy. The average person has around 10 pounds of material in their intestine at all times. If it feels like you are constantly on the toilet with this program—Good! The point is to empty out the organs to give everything a rest and to return proper peristalsis in the intestine.

For the days prior to any fast we recommend stimulating more bowel movements. Three or four is a good number. Use a product that combines magnesium with oxygen, like Oxy-Mag brand, see *Resources,* p. 255, or use an herbal laxative like Swiss-Kriss that you can find in your health food store. Drink plenty of pear juice or *Prune Juice* (see recipe, p. 190).

Remember to avoid a diarrhea condition for more than a day. In that case, slow the laxatives and add 2 heaping tablespoons of fresh ground flax meal to each beverage you have. Slow down on fruit beverages and go for vegetable-based beverages and soup. It's a good thing to remember the "better out than in" rule, and also know how to stop a cleanse if you need to. This is in cases of extreme frailty. Generally speaking, LifeFood Nutritional Fasting with the raw blended soups will help to stabilize the situation. You can always mash half an avocado into soup to slow the cleanse.

OUTLINING THE 14-DAY FAST

DAYS 1, 2, & 3: *Non-Flushing Days*

LifeFood Nutritional Fast with LifeFood beverages and soups

- AM: smoothie

- NOON: soup and nut milk

- PM: soup and green drink

Drink plenty of fluids and all the LifeFood beverages that you want. You shouldn't feel hungry at all during the fast.

- SNACKS: each day make a different beverage to take with you and keep sipping on. Pick any from the *What To Have* list (see p. 219).

- 3 vitamin packs per day: AM, NOON, PM (see p. 226).

- 3 castor packs per day (see p. 229).

Stimulate 3–4 bowel movements per day, using the laxatives of your choice. This will greatly soften the hard outer coating of the bile stones, making it very comfortable to pass them. (See *What To Have,* p. 219).

DAY 4: *Gallbladder Flush* (see p. 224).

Stick to juices and nut milk until after you've had your oil. You don't want the oil hung up by digesting soup or thick smoothies.

DAYS 5, 6, & 7: *Non-flushing Days*

Follow same regimen as Non-flushing Days 1, 2, & 3.

DAY 8: *Liver Flush #1*

Like the Gallbladder Flush, with only 4–6 ounces of oil. (See *Liver Flush,* p. 226.)

DAYS 9 & 10: *Non-flushing Days*

Follow same regimen as Non-flushing Days 1, 2, & 3.

DAY 11: *Liver Flush #2*

Stop taking Ortho-Phos drops

Discontinue castor packs (or keep going if you like)

Continue drinking LifeFood Nutritional Fast beverages

Take 3 vitamin packs per day

DAYS 12 & 13: *Non-flushing Days*

Follow same regimen as Non-flushing Days 1, 2, & 3.

DAY 14: BREAK THE FAST

See Star*ting & Breaking the Fast*, p. 221. You may feel like continuing the fast; it's safe to continue as long as you like as long as you keep lots of LifeFood beverages hydrating and nourishing your body. Should you decide to continue, do 1–2 flushes per week, either gallbladder or liver flush, as you see fit.

GALLBLADDER FLUSH—DAY 4

- Begin the day as a usual non-flushing day.

- Take bacteria upon rising.

- Take a vitamin pack with nut milk for breakfast.

- You may want to increase your laxatives to insure a good bowel movement or two before drinking your oil.

- Do a *Castor Pack* (see p. 229).

- Have thinner beverage and avoid thick smoothies or soup until later.

- Prepare for your flush by fixing your Coffee Enema and juicing your lemon juice (1 cup). Set out olive oil (8–12 ounces) and enzymes.

Drinking the Oil

At approximately 1:30 in the afternoon, begin to sip 8–10 ounces of olive oil, alternately sipping 1 cup of straight fresh lemon juice.

Consume them both within an hour. Take 5–10 enzymes (open the capsules into your mouth and let the powder dissolve).

Doing the Castor Pack

Prepare a Castor Pack, relax and lay down for a while. It's good to lie on the right side of your body. A cup of peppermint or ginger tea will soothe the tummy. After a half an hour, take 5 more enzymes in the same way. Repeat every 15–30 minutes until nausea is completely relieved. Bacteria also works well here if you happen to run out of enzymes. Open 3 capsules into mouth and let dissolve. After your Castor Pack, prepare your Coffee Enema. The Castor Pack process should take at least an hour.

Do a Coffee Enema

Evoke a powerful cleanse by taking a coffee enema (see *How To Do an Enema*, p. 232). Relax and go about your day. Plan to have this day and the next one easy and restful where you can be at home. Relax after the coffee enema by lying on your right side with a pillow under your hips.

The Harvest

In 8–15 hours, or the next morning and right through out the next day, you'll begin to pass the stones. The average person on a cooked food diet can expect to pass 50–200 or more stones ranging in size from little flakes of what is referred to as gravel, to small pea size, to thumbnail size. Even large stones the size of a horse chestnut are passed effortlessly. You'll continue to pass stones for the next few bowel movements, and perhaps even beyond that. Another enema can be performed the next morning to empty the intestine and further flush stones and debris.

The stones will range in color from yellow, emerald green, dark green, to black, often with a strong odor. Better out than in! The stones can be collected through a sieve, rinsed and stored capped in a glass jar in the freezer to show your like-minded friends. Digestion greatly improves with this simple procedure. Most will experience optimal results by doing many Gallbladder and Liver Flushes. Do your next flush once you feel rested and ready to do more cleansing.

For Stubborn Stones—Potentiate Your Flush

Drink 1–2 teaspoons Epson Salt, found in drug stores, with 8 ounces of water. This will act in union with the Gallbladder Flush to create soap-like action in the digestive tract. Take the Epson salt after you've finished drinking the oil and lemon juice. Epson salt can be taken at any time that a laxative is needed, and used externally, an Epson salt bath can bring much relief and promote detoxification through the skin, the largest eliminative organ in the body.

LIVER FLUSH—DAYS 8 & 11

The Liver Flush is exactly the same as the Gallbladder Flush with only one difference—less oil is consumed. Only drink 4–6 ounces of oil for the Liver Flush. Follow directions as outlined in the Gallbladder Flush. It is also recommended for the Liver Flush that you consume only light beverages before drinking the oil, since a heavy soup or smoothie might slow up the oil from getting to where we want it, saturating the liver rather than hanging out in the upper stomach for any length of time. Most people feel like continuing with light beverages for the rest of the day regardless because the sensation of having the oil in them feels unusual enough. However, if you feel like a soup later on, then by all means have it.

DAILY VITAMIN PACKS

We recommend making 3 vitamin packs for each day. Besides the laxatives and the orthophosphoric acid, these vitamins are not required but rather recommended. If 3 packs is too much for you, then only take 2 per day. This helps make your fast easier and supports the immune system during this time. You can be creative as to what goes in; however, we recommend these basics:

Required

   2–5 Oxy-Mag (or Oxy-Oxc) laxative

   2–5 Swiss Kriss herbal laxative

   30 drops Orthophosphoric acid (or 1 tablespoon raw apple cider vinegar)

   Optional and recommended:

   500 mg. Niacinamide (Vitamin B3, non-flushing type)

   200 mg. Vitamin B6, B12, Folic Acid (MegaFoods brand)

   125 mg. Magnesium (MegaFoods brand)

   100 mg. Chromium GTF (MegaFoods brand)

Take these 3 times a day. Take 1 vitamin pack in the morning when you rise and are up and about. Take one at noon with your soup. Take the last one around 6pm. Always take nutritional vitamins with a Life-Food beverage or a soup.

NOTE: All supplements can be ordered if you can't find them locally.
(See Resources, *p. 255.)*

Bacteria—Another Good Thing to Take

Generally, we recommend taking a good probiotic bacteria strain. Kyodophillus is good and readily available at your health food store. Take the recommended amount first thing upon rising, on an empty stomach, with water. Let it culture within you, taking no other nutrients for the next 20 minutes to an hour. This practice can continue long after the fast for better digestion and colon irrigation.

HOW RECOMMENDED VITAMINS ARE USED DURING THE FAST

Oxy-Mag or Oxy-Oxc: A powerful laxative. Take Oxy-Mag up to 4 times per day to keep bowels moving. Follow directions on label. It's best with charged water with lemon. Adjust dose as necessary.

Swiss Kriss: An herbal laxative. Take up to 5 tablets 3 or 4 times per day to promote 4 bowel movements per day for 2–3 days prior to the fast. Adjust dosage if necessary.

Ortho-Phosphoric Acid: Breaks down bile stones. Take 30 drops 3 times per day for the first 8 days, or substitute 1 tablespoon of raw apple cider vinegar and take 4 times per day instead. This softens the hardened mucous and inorganic minerals in body organs. Take for 3 days prior to doing any liver or gallbladder flush to potentiate your flush.

Magnesium: Opens up over 300 detoxification pathways in the body. It is burned through quickly when doing a lot of mental activity. Magnesium is nature's tranquilizer and relaxes the muscles with its gentle laxative quality.

Niacinamide, Vitamin B3: Promotes circulation in the body. We used to recommend the flushing type of niacin, and now we like the niacinamide better because you can take it in greater amounts right from the start, instead of having to work yourself up. Most people are lacking niacin; this is a good time to stock up on this important vitamin.

Vitamin B6, B12, Folic Acid: Stress and daily fatigue deplete us of these vitamins. This is a wonderful time to top up on these nutrients. Any muscle fatigue, such as carpel tunnel syndrome, is relieved with this trio of vitamins. Dream recall is dependent upon sufficient supplies of Vitamin B6.

Chromium GTF: This important mineral helps heal an overtaxed pancreas from a life of sugary starches. It helps sugar-sensitive people deal with fruit beverages.

Broad Spectrum Enzymes: Take these after the oil has been consumed in the gallbladder and liver flushes. Take the powder (open capsules if you have them in caps) directly onto your tongue. This will break down the oil and get it out of your upper stomach in record time so it saturates the liver and gallbladder. This is where we want the oil to go, and the sooner the better. Take 5 capsules every 15–30 minutes until all nausea is resolved.

CASTOR PACKS

Supplies needed: 1 cup (or more) castor oil, wool or cotton flannel, plastic wrap, and a hot water bottle or heating pad. Wool and cotton flannel is found in stores sold with castor oil. Fold your flannel so that it is long enough to reach from the bottom line of the breast to the top of your pelvic bone. It should be wide enough to go from the side of your ribcage (about where the arm hangs at rest) to your midline (bellybutton). Holding your flannel in one hand pour about half a cup of castor oil on the flannel and spread it out. Add more until that side of flannel is saturated with castor oil. Apply over mid-section of body, especially over the liver (right side of abdomen, lower ribcage). In order to hold this in place and to keep castor from leaking over clothes and sofa, take plastic wrap, like Saran Wrap, and make a corset by winding it around your trunk 2 or 3 times, making sure to go low enough at the bottom to protect your pants. Wrapping a clinging plastic wrap around your entire waist a few times comfortably holds flannel and castor oil in place. Castor oil is absorbed by the body faster when heat is applied, so put your feet up and apply a hot water bottle or heating pad over the pack. Put a few towels or a blanket on to insulate the whole thing. This simple process brings a great healing to the liver while it will loosen and soften stones and engage the lymph system. It is recommended to do 2–3 per day, 30–60 minutes each, especially up to the last flush on Day 11. Castor packs are healing whenever you can do them, so do as many as you can. The hot water bottle should be comfortable to the skin; never fill hot water bottles with boiling water. Always fill from a hot tap. Put a towel around your hot water bottle if it's too hot to the skin.

Secret Teaching: The castor bean is called the "palm of Christ" or the "giving oil" for its miraculous healing properties. Castor packs can be placed over all parts of the body to bring relief to backaches, neck trauma, sprains, broken bones, carpel tunnel, rashes from plants and insects, dry skin conditions, eliminating warts, psoriasis, and other conditions. It is in many skin lotions and in our after bath body oil (see Secret Dakini After-Bath Body Oil, *p. 212). Castor oil can be used internally to boost the immune system, generally 1 tablespoon per day is recommended.*

Supply List

Tools

- Vita-Mix, or Blender
- Grinder for seeds, electric coffee grinder works well

- Hot Water Bottle/Enema Bag (a combination bag is best)
- Castor Oil with wool or cotton flannel
- Clinging plastic wrap, like Saran Wrap, for castor pack

Oil

- Organic Olive Oil: Finest quality, for drinking during flushes
- Flax Seed Oil with Borage: by LER, for use in soup, smoothies, etc.
- Coconut Butter: Omega brand, for use in soup, smoothies, etc.

Supplements

- Enzymes: broad-spectrum enzymes with high lipase content
- Ortho-Phosphoric Acid, or raw apple cider vinegar
- Optional and Recommended: Niacin-Vitamin B3, Chromium GTF, Magnesium, Vitamin B6, B12, Folic Acid, Kyodophillus (or other good probiotic)

Laxatives

- Oxy-Mag
- Swiss Kriss

Organics from the Health Food Store

- Tree-ripened lemons, 1 cup fresh juice for each flush, with more lemons for soup and *Electrolyte Lemonade*
- Organic coffee, for enema
- Celtic sea salt (sun-dried), for minerals, electrolytes
- Miso (unpasteurized), for stimulating digestive juices
- Ground raw seeds: flax, pumpkin, sesame, for hormones and to act like a broom, sweeping out the intestinal tract

- Ginger, cayenne, garlic: blood-movers
- Raw honey: be modest with all sugar, 2 tablespoons per day is enough
- Dulse flakes: for soups; provides iodine, vitamin B12, B6, etc.
- Fresh raw fruit and vegetables, nuts and seeds

HOW TO DO AN ENEMA

8 cups charged water
Enema bag

First prepare the water. Use room temperature water, or you can have your water at body temperature. For fancy enemas, slow brew herbal combinations, straining the water well. Read in an herbal book about different medicinal herbs. Catnip, for example, is very soothing. Marshmallow root can bring relief to hemorrhoids and ruptured blood vessels.

Prepare the enema bag by filling it with water and hanging it at a height of approximately 3½–5 feet off the floor. Hanging it higher moves the water too fast, and can create unnecessary pressure on the bowel. Do it either in the bathtub or on the floor, making yourself comfortable with several towels. Remove any air in the hose of the enema bag by allowing water to come down to the clip, then clip it off. Most enema hoses are somewhat transparent so you can see where the liquid is. Lubricate the nozzle with a small dab of organic hair conditioner, or an all-natural salve.

Enema Procedure and Technique

Get on all fours; raise your buttocks up, with your heart to the earth. Insert nozzle gently, then slowly unclip enema hose to release a little water at a time. Go slowly, so you are comfortable. Add more as you relax. A normal adult will be able to take in the entire amount.

The abdomen can be massaged to take the water higher. Start at the lower abdomen. Massage up and to the left side of your body. Then move across the middle (just below belly button area) and over to the right side.

Hold the water in as long as is comfortable. Five to fifteen minutes is good. You'll be comfortable holding it longer as enemas become a regular practice. Always be kind and gentle with yourself. Release into the toilet. It will probably come out in waves, releasing debris.

> *IMPORTANT NOTE: Enemas will flush the bowel of important bacteria, so it is important to reseed the intestinal flora when completing a series of enemas. Reseed the bowel by implanting an acidophilus culture like L-Salivarius, Master Blend, or Kyo-dophilus (found in stores). Dissolve 10 capsules acidophilus into 2–3 ounces of charged water. Let this culture in a bowl for a few hours and then insert into the colon with a baby enema bag. Move and massage it up through the intestine by manipulating the abdominal region and go straight to bed. Keep it in until morning. These types of acidophilus are the kind that actually implants, reseeding the flora. Other transient types are beneficial because they live a life cycle, then become food for us. The L-Salivarius and Kyo-dophilus actually reseed.*

Ways Around the Enema

You can book a session with a colon hydro therapist if you prefer. Colonics are a great way to ensure complete evacuation of the intestine. If you schedule it for the day after, though, you may miss seeing all the cool stones that come out of you. If you do have a colonic, inform your practitioner of your recent flush and to look for gallstones. Look for a practitioner who understands the importance of reseeding the intestine and implants good, quality bacteria at the end of the session.

COFFEE ENEMA

¼ cup organic coffee grounds for every 8 cups charged water

Grind coffee and place it in charged (purified or distilled) water at room temperature overnight. Carefully strain out all grounds with cloth and a strainer. Follow enema instructions. The coffee enema works well in union with the Gallbladder Flush as it stimulates the dumping of bile from the liver. Coffee taken in this way has the opposite effect as when taken orally. Here it dilates the gall ducts, stimulating bile secretions.

Why Flush?

This is a rather aggressive way to deal with our rather radical twentieth-century dietary habits. Nearly everyone has gallstones, people who have had their gallbladders removed yet continue to eat processed food will continue to develop gallstones that will pack into the bile ducts. Autopsies on small children reveal gallstones. Gallstones are initially formed of insipid pus, bile pigments, calcium salts, and cholesterol. They are usually found extending the shape of a packed gallbladder. Bile flow must occur between or through these stones and gravel. Save yourself money and pain down the line and do an occasional Gallbladder Flush.

What's Next?

Most people will need to do between 10 and 15 Gallbladder Flushes to empty the organ. Consider doing several 14-Day LifeFood Nutritional Fasts each year until you are stone-free. After several Gallbladder Flushes, it would be good to consider starting the Parasite Flush.

100-DAY PARASITE FLUSH

1 ounce green black walnut

1 ounce wormwood

1 ounce clove

1 ounce quassia

½ ounce male fern

A great follow up treatment after the Gallbladder Flush. Since parasites breed in gallstones it is generally recommended to do several Gallbladder Flushes before beginning the Parasite Flush. Grind all herbs to a powder. The quassia is a very sturdy shredded bark and will need extra grinding (a Vita-Mixer works well). The other herbs can be finely ground in a regular grinder. Mix together well. Keep sealed in a glass container in the refrigerator, or a dark cool place. Or just get the formula premixed from our LifeFood order line (see *Resources,* p. 255).

Dosage

For adults: Take 1 level teaspoon 2 times daily for best results.

For children and house pets: Take ½–⅓ teaspoon once a day and according to size. Mix it into a few ounces of raw apple juice/cider. Take for 100 days to eliminate a broad range of parasites, worms, and their eggs. The clove makes it taste really yummy. Chew it well as major absorption to the brain occurs when herbs are chewed well with plenty of saliva. After 100 days of following the above routine, take a maintenance dose. For adults: 1 level teaspoon once or twice a week; for children and pets: ½–⅓ dosage, according to size.

It is said that approximately 80% of the world population have parasites and worms. Virtually everyone who has pets and children has some sort of parasites or worms. Ever see a small filament float across your eye lens? Probably worms. Many of today's most common maladies are as a result of, or compounded by, the presence of parasites and worms.

We'll save the horror stories about these microscopic vermin and suffice it to say that it's a wonderful feeling to be cleansed of the little buggers. Read up on the subject. Become educated and shape your lifestyle to be parasite-free. The above recipe to flush them is highly effective when used for 100 days. This completes the egg-laying cycle and is effective in eliminating over 100 different types of parasites and worms.

CLEANSE WITH ENZYMES & SPIRULINA

Enzymes and spirulina are two nutritive supplements that can dissolve body sludge and make you feel better and stronger than ever. Enzymes are involved in every single function in the body. The vast majority of people today have spent their whole lives eating a diet of cooked food that is depleted of enzymes. The cleaning power of a broad-spectrum enzyme supplement combined with the awesome protein of spirulina will cleanse the body and restore health.

There are a few different kinds of sugar, about nine different types of fat. However, there are over 20,000 different possible combinations of protein. Protein forms the building blocks of our whole body and its process. The vast majority of the people of the earth have developed enzyme-resistant protein linkages as a result of having eaten proteins that are de-natured by cooking. These types of proteins become congealed and coagulated, making them less than water-soluble.

Everything has to be miscible with water that is taken into the body, and protein should be able to be broken down into single amino acids. There is a combination of some 26 or more amino acids that make up the 20,000 variations of protein that compose every inch of you—from your bones to the tissue of the eyes that you gaze through. Proteins act as carrying agents that make metabolites miscible in the body's fluids. Most people need to strengthen their stomach acid and pepsin secretions, which start the process of breaking down protein into single amino acids.

Taking enzyme supplements with an excellent source of protein like blue green algae can give your body a maximal boost to restore vitality. Plant-based enzymes have a much wider pH range; this is one reason why plant protein is far superior to animal protein. Spirulina is one of the most complete sources of protein on the face of the earth. It is rich in phycotine pigments, minerals, anti-oxidants, trace elements and other nutritive components including magnesium. Magnesium is integral in more than 300 detox pathways of the body and helps us to relax, often referred to as nature's tranquilizer. Chlorophyll and blood are much alike. Unbeknownst to most, blood is in fact formed in the intestinal villa from the food substrate called monora. Most of our cells in the body arrive from having originally been an ethrocyte (red blood cell). Digestion is primary in restoring vitality.

A therapeutic dose of enzymes (see instructions) taken with Spirulina can help the immune system rid the body of candida, and clear waste in the tissues of the body, improving arthritic and rheumatic conditions, often in a matter of a few days! Digestive enzymes are carried by the white blood cells through the lymphatic system and can break down materials to a state that can be carried out of the body.

THERAPEUTIC DOSE OF ENZYMES & SPIRULINA

Begin with high-quality products. For enzymes, we like Life Enhancement Resources Hi-Zimes; for Spirulina, try Spirulina Pacifica tablets by Nutrex or Crystal Flakes (Spirulina flakes with Lecithin) by Nutrex.

A therapeutic dose consists of taking 10 Hi-Zymes per hour for 10 hours in a day (100 enzymes per day), combined with Spirulina (take 3 tablets, about ½ teaspoon, of algae per 10 enzymes each hour). On this program a tooth abscess can clear in 3 days; major candida can clear in 7 days; chronic conditions like chronic fatigue, stiff joints, muscle spasm, and chronic back pain may take longer (up to 30 days). Those with stomach ulcers or pregnant women should choose a milder dose.

The enzymes to use are broad-spectrum enzymes that split proteins (Protease), fats (Lipase), carbohydrates (Cellulase, Maltase, and Sucrase), sugars (Amylase), and dairy (Lactase). This program is safe and is recommended for a period of up to 30 days for internal cleansing, especially for people who have quite a bit of tissue cleansing to do and want to speed up the process. It is most effective when used in conjunction with Jubbs 14-Day LifeFood Nutritional Fast. Imagine if you cleaned your house every day for some days running! How clean would your house be after two days? Five days? A person would typically use this program for one week, or until they experience relief from their ailment. As always, apply common sense and discontinue if adverse symptoms were to arise, any pain.

We've consulted many people with chronic fatigue, cancer, candida, parasites, and a host of other modern day conditions to cleanse their system with a program of LifeFood nutrition and juicing, flax and bee pollen, and the therapeutic dose of enzymes combined with Spirulina and watched them become radiant in a matter of a few weeks! The skin becomes more elastic, wrinkles soften and disappear, pores of the face become smaller, and a healthy pallor is regained. You'll feel energetic and look incredible. The enzymes will help the immune system break down necrosed material. Enzymes are carried by the white blood cells through the lymphatic system to clear and clean.

CHAPTER 11

THE ABCs
OF LIFEFOOD NUTRITION

LIFEFOOD NUTRITION

LifeFood nutrition is fresh, raw fruits and vegetables, organic and in-season when possible; sprouted seeds, nuts, and legumes, along with some fermented foods that are properly combined for easy digestion. Life-Food has a life force that can be measured in many ways, such as with Kirlean photography. LifeFood is always raw, always alive, and also contains its enzymes, a life force, which means that there are minerals and other components to the food that our body can easily digest, assimilate, and utilize. LifeFood is wild food, which is found growing wild in nature or with some semblance of itself found growing outside of the farmer's fence. LifeFood is vegetarian, and mainly vegan, congruent with the philosophy that our food choices promote a sustainable future for our planet.

EXCITOTOXINS

Excitotoxins are food additives that dangerously excite the neurons of the brain. By now most of us have heard that MSG, an excitotoxin, is less than healthy. Monosodium Glutamate, or MSG, was created in a laboratory around the turn of the century and has since turned into a multi-billion-dollar industry. MSG has the ability to mask bland, tasteless food, making it taste delicious. MSG is found in chips, canned food, frozen food, fast food, diet food, baby food, as well as the soups and sauces sold in most restaurants. In America, MSG use has doubled every decade since the 1940s. MSG and related excitotoxins are often disguised on packaged food labels under names like: "hydrolyzed vegetable protein," "vegetable protein," "natural flavorings," and "spices." Each of these may contain from 12%–40% MSG!

Hydrolyzed vegetable protein and texturized vegetable protein (TVP) are made through several unnatural chemical processes. First, rotten and bruised vegetables are boiled in sulfuric acid for hours, then the acid is neutralized with caustic soda (an alkaline agent used to make soap), and then the brown sludge is scraped off and dried to a fine brown powder. MSG is often added to this. Analysis of this very modern taste enhancer reveals that it contains three very powerful brain cell toxins (glutamate, aspartate, and cystic acid), as well as several known carcinogens (cancer-causing substances). This product poses an even *greater* threat than MSG!

MSG and other excitotoxins like aspartate (aspartame), a main ingredient in artificial sweeteners, may cause severe damage to the neurons in the retina of the eye, along with widespread destruction of neurons in the hypothalamus and other memory-related areas of the brain. Newborns and young children are most at risk; many formulas and packaged baby foods are loaded with excitotoxins so babies will innocently consume them. Excitotoxins are especially harmful to the developing child (fetus, pregnant mother) and are known to cause legions in the hypothalamus of the brain. The hypothalamus is responsible for regulating growth, the onset of puberty, proper function of the endocrine glands, normal appetite, as well as regulating sleep cycles and waking patterns.

By cloaking the now recognized MSG name on food labels, much of the public is fooled to believe that "natural flavors" are natural. Beware! Avoid these products! An excellent resource book to read on this subject is *Excitotoxins: The Taste That Kills,* by Russell L. Blaylock, M.D. (Santa Fe: Health Press, 1994).

DHEA

Plants contain saponins and sterol-like complexes that are similar to body counterparts in structure. They fit into sterol and prostiglandin (hormones that act locally) dehydrogenase enzymes and receptor sites. DHEA and other hormones are found in abundance in the 20-year-old, with a rapid downhill slide after the age of 25. The typical 80-year-old is often found to have 5% of what the 20-year-old has.

We recommend that both men and women who need more hormones take a supplement of wild yam that includes the amino acids L-argenine and L-lysine. Everyone can benefit from this practice, particularly women going through menopause. Artificial estrogens pharmaceuticals mimic our own body hormones, though with a major difference.

Pharmaceutical estrogens are created in the laboratory to be unique to the pharmaceutical company rather than nature. It must be unique for a patent to be obtained. No patent can be obtained for an herb. Pharmaceutical hormones fit receptor sites in the body designed for natural hormones. These designer hormones become lodged in the receptor sites and bog down the natural flow that would occur. Use all-natural herbs or food-grown supplements. There are two very good brands on the market: Pro-Plus, by RX Group, and Empress Plus. (See *Whole Food Vitamin & Mineral Supplements,* p. 245.)

YOUR LIFEFOOD PET

All animals that live in the wild eat their meals raw. It is an exclusively human trait to cook food and feed it to animals. Animals in the wild die of old age, while domesticated animals now mimic very human maladies and disease. We wouldn't eat canned and dry food only, yet I often see people feeding the animals just that. Animals love LifeFood! When it is prepared with their special needs taken into account, a Life-Food pet will astound your friends with its white teeth and gleaming coat. LifeFood cats and dogs have little fat, no dandruff, and don't shed much. Animal-allergy sufferers can often sit comfortably near LifeFood pets and remark on how rare this situation is.

Not ready to go all the way to LifeFood with your pet? Even if your pet is still eating out of a can you can improve their health by sprinkling some spirulina over their food. One tablespoon of the flakes, or less if it is condensed (half that for a smaller animal), is a good dosage. You can add some powdered enzymes to the dead canned food and at least give them something to work it down with. Add 1 tablespoon of flax seed oil or any good oil to their food and their coats will become very shiny. If you have access to happy chickens you can break a raw egg onto their food (a whole egg for a large animal and just the yoke for smaller ones) to perk up their coats and give them a boost of enzymes. A raw egg has over 200 different enzymes. Add some MSM powder to their water for supple muscles and joints. Our cats have always liked to chew up certain whole food vitamin complexes like the chromium, Vitamin E, and the B6, B12, folic acid complex and I've seen dogs munch them up, too. Little patches of wheatgrass are sold at Farmers Markets for cats. They love the grass and its good for them; just sprinkle a little water on it to keep it green and growing. Cats love catnip, fresh or dried. Nothing perks up the home like a cat enraptured in catnip magic. Especially for housebound animals, it is important to create excitement for them on a regular basis to simulate a more natural life. In other words, be creative. Your pet will really appreciate it.

DOG FOOD

Dogs love soft fruit and super smoothies for breakfast and huge salads that are chopped up well (dogs lack molars for grinding) and tossed with a LifeFood sauce. Add crunchy romaine lettuce, ½–1 avocado, a tomato, shredded carrot, fresh-ground nuts (like almonds) or seeds (sesame or pumpkin), brewers or nutritional yeast, a sea vegetable (powdered kelp or dulse), a sprinkle of a product like Vegi-Dog (a mineral supplement), and then toss with a dressing like Tahini Tamari. Dogs love apples, plums, apples, berries, and avocados.

Dogs appreciate a good sauce, too. We usually toss a few vegetables into the blender, say a cup of cucumber and a cup of red pepper, then season it with tahini, a good oil, Bragg Liquid Aminos, any left over salad or vegetable juice or Rejuvelac, and a little spirulina and blend well. We toss this with salad and serve. Remember, always soak seeds first and grind them to make sure they'll get digested and assimilated well. Blend soaked seeds and nuts with your dressing/sauce. It's good to do sunflower seeds this way.

CAT FOOD

Cats love plain avocado, tomato, or cucumber—peeled and diced up finely. Sprinkle nutritional or brewers yeast, add a few drops of Bragg Liquid Aminos, and a good oil. Then sprinkle kelp powder and spirulina over it. Cats love colostrum, goat's whey, sprouts, and fresh catnip.

There are products like Vegi-Cat, a mineral supplement for cats, at health stores. Add a bit of that and toss well. Always remember to chop things up into small pieces for your cat, since they lack grinding molars. Cats love melon and fresh-ground coconut meat!

LIGHT

A vast majority of the light (some say up to 90%) that we take in enters the body through the eyes. This light is essential in setting all of the body's diurnal cycles. The sun's ultraviolet spectrum is blocked out by glass, and as a result many people today are light deficient, also known as malillumination. Windows in the home and car, sunglasses, contact lenses, and eyeglasses all inhibit the eye from taking in this essential nutrient—full-spectrum light. At least 1 hour of sunlight per day (no glasses or contact lenses) is recommended. You can be in the shade; simply take in the light.

CLEAN WATER TO DRINK AND BATHE IN

Today most every town and city adds chemicals to their water supply. Two top toxins are chlorine and fluoride. Get a reverse-osmosis water filter to purify your own fresh, clear, clean water from your tap (see *High Alkaline Charged Water,* p. 41). One 5-minute shower can be like drinking several glasses of unpurified chlorinated water. Get a shower filter to purify the water you bathe in. Fill your tub through your filter for your bath.

A favorite quote from Nikola Tesla, the late great scientist of this century, when asked in the 1950s about his predictions for the next 100 years was, "...only a lunatic would drink unpurified water."

Chlorine: Binds with the protein of the hair and skin, making hair dry and brittle. We take in the most chlorine when we bathe.

Fluoride: First introduced to the human water supply during World War II. It was used in the Nazi and Russian prison camps to keep the population docile and to not question authority. It makes one curious about its effect on our population, doesn't it? The type of fluoride that is commonly added to city water is a by-product of aluminum smelting and is to be avoided.

Aluminum: Avoid all aluminum products, i.e., all aluminum soda cans, cooking pots and pans, aluminum foil, many commercial toothpastes, and underarm antiperspirants, as most all contain aluminum (see *Antiperspirant & Breast Health,* p. 211). Aluminum is a manmade metal and lingers in the tissue. Alzheimer's patients are found to have large amounts of aluminum in their brain tissue. All life has an energetic force that spins in a clockwise direction. Aluminum spins in the opposite direction. Remove all aluminum products from your life.

WHOLE FOOD VITAMIN & MINERAL SUPPLEMENTS

We highly recommend the use of whole food vitamin and mineral complex supplements, vitamin and mineral supplements that are derived from whole food sources (i.e., grown on yeast so they are naturally chelated and complete with their complement/companion elements). Yeast acts like a gateway from the mineral kingdom. We cannot just chew a bit of iron and get the benefit. Our body builds iron, from its constituent parts, on demand.

Most vitamin and mineral supplements are really just drugs and are useless as far as we are concerned. However, if they are whole food supplements they can be very beneficial to correct nutritional deficiency. For example, magnesium is involved in over 300 detoxification pathways in the body. It is estimated that some 80% of Americans are magnesium deficient. Most of us have a lifetime of the typical American diet of cooked food behind us, and to truly gain optimum health we'd have to consume incredible amounts of food to top up our nutritional level of vitamins and minerals.

We biologically transmutate what we need through the building blocks of nutrition supplied in whole foods. Whole food supplements should be chewed well to gain maximum absorption into the head. They are quite tasty—even your pet will like to chew them up. The product brands that we use are Life Enhancement Resources and MegaFoods; Rainbow Light also has a living line of vitamins, and LifeStar is also excellent. All whole food supplements will say so on the label. Settle for nothing less. Can't find them in your health store?

Order supplements and all Jubb-recommended products for health, body, and home from Jubbs LONGEVITY store. (See *Resources*, p. 255.)

3 THINGS MOST PEOPLE NEED MORE OF

1. Essential Fatty Acids: 100% of people checked are deficient in essential fatty acids. (See *Cold-pressed Oil*, p. 53.)

Sources:

- Cold-pressed seed or nut oil, 2 or 3 tablespoons per day
- Shiny seeds and nuts ground to a meal
- Coconut butter is an excellent source.

2. Pyridoxine, Vitamin B6: 92% of people checked are deficient in Vitamin B6. Healthy intestines produce it. Men especially need more B6 and can benefit from a high-quality food grown vitamin B6 supplement. Carpal tunnel syndrome can be greatly relieved with a B6 supplement. B6 is required for our ability to recall dreams. Dream recall is normal so take B6 until dream recall resumes.

Sources

- Sea vegetables
- Whole grains
- Whole food vitamin supplement

3. Magnesium: 96% of people checked are deficient in magnesium. Magnesium is nature's tranquilizer. It keeps us calm and serene. Magnesium is essential to many of the detox pathways of the body. If magnesium is deficient, the pathways can bottleneck and nothing moves until more magnesium arrives. Magnesium deficiency is chronic in America. Stress and pollution call for extra doses of magnesium.

Sources

- All dark leafy greens

- Alfalfa

- Parsley

- Dulse

- Dandelion greens

- Primrose

- Whole food mineral supplement

ESSENTIAL FATTY ACIDS: LIVING OIL

Some say why use oil at all? On a typical American diet with huge quantities of empty food and gallons of sugar water beverages, the average American 20-year-old has a 20% occlusion (plaque) to the major arteries supplying blood to the heart. The body will usually allow up to a 90% occlusion before feeling the sensation of angina.

Most of us have consumed buckets of dead "motor" oil—oil that is heated past 360 degrees Fahrenheit to let it keep on the supermarket shelf for years and years. No animal will eat that oil, except for humans who should be educated with cigarette-type warning labels. It is totally dead and loaded with detergents, deodorants, and bleaches. The essential fatty acids in those oils are completely destroyed. Dangerous trans-fatty acids and free-radicals would have been consumed. When you see those oils in the supermarket, project the skull and crossbones onto the containers and know them for what they are—Toxic!

The body finds it less than possible to break down dead oil. With each onslaught of deep fried food, french fries, and rancid ranch salad dressing, the body does what it can to pack those rancid oils away—into the vein and artery walls, colon, and joints.

Really high-quality oil, especially flax seed, coconut, and pumpkin seed oil, can greatly aid the recovering body in the transition to LifeFood nutrition. These live oils enter the system and go to work to create a structure within the body to help clear and clean the plaque that lines the artery walls. Coconut butter and flax seed oil are best. Rich in essential fatty acids with a good omega–6 to –3 ratio, they help to rejuvenate the toxic body by making the blood more slippery. Two or three tablespoons per day is recommended. There are many fat-soluble vitamins and minerals and trace minerals that are absorbed more readily in the presence of good essential fatty acids. In a short while, one begins to notice an amazing change in the elasticity of the skin throughout the body.

Good oil is much more expensive than dead oil because the process is done slowly with high-quality materials. This oil will rinse away with water. Dead oil will cling to whatever it touches. The live oil is water soluble when still bound with its protein carrier. The more raw (less refined) the better.

To reduce cholesterol and clear lipids and plaque from the body, one can combine flax seed oil with bee pollen as a snack.

SEA VEGETABLES

In the last 100 years we've lost 75% of our topsoil through poor farming practices and clear cutting forests. Many of the soils precious trace minerals have been blown or washed away and are now in the ocean. Eating sea vegetables is a great way to stock up on these essential minerals and trace minerals, especially iodine. Iodine in itself can combat obesity by feeding the thyroid into action to help metabolize fats. Kelp is rich with iodine. Use it in its granulated form for seasoning salads and sandwiches. Dulse is also a favorite table condiment that contains iodine. We very often put a bowl of dried (as they come from the store) or soaked seaweed on the table. The sea vegetables are yummy, slightly salty, and satisfy in the way toasted corn chips did in the past. Read more about Sea Vegetables in the *Definition of Terms*, p. 49.

HONEY, BEE POLLEN, & PROPOLYS

Honey: Do you really know what honey is? Honey is the sexual fluid of the flowers and plants processed by bees for us. The worker bees keep busy to maintain their hive and supply a surplus of honey. Honey is actually the clear nectar of flowers. This nectar is collected by the bees and brought back to the hive where the many bees, in unison, vibrate their wings to evaporate the nectar. As the water dissolves, the nectar thickens and takes on more of its characteristic golden color. Good honey contains enzymes from the bees, particles of pollen, propolys and other waxes, resins, and bee parts.

Honey is high in potassium and in its raw state can help heal. It helps alkalize the body and acts like a diuretic to help reduce water retention. Of all foods eaten, honey is one of the few that supplies us with a surplus of enzymes beyond what is needed to break the honey down.

Pollen: Bee pollen is also a high-energy whole food that supplies us with most everything we need. It is a very high grade of protein—one of the highest you can get. We often fast on apples and bee pollen for days, even weeks. If you need to heal, bee pollen might be recommended. It is one of the richest foods with very few calories. Bee pollen is rich in lysine and structurally is made from a very long chain of amino acids that are easily broken down by the body into single amino acids. It is super food.

Many people experience relief from seasonal allergies by introducing small amounts of fresh, local pollen to their diet. Pollen is the sperm of the flowers, grasses, and trees and contains within it all of the plant's hormones.

Propolys: Propolys is used by bees to make the hive antiseptic. Mice have been found, centuries-old and perfectly preserved from the day they were stung to death, sealing their fate and encasing them in propolys. The unfortunate mouse may have crawled into the hive to secure some honey and was probably stung to death. In this case, bees cannot remove the mouse, so they opt to mummify it in propolys to preserve the hygiene of the hive. Propolys is the resin of the tree carefully collected by the diligent worker bee.

Propolys is sold in the herb store, usually as a hard resin; high-quality propolys is soft and chewable. It is often very hard so grate the resin and spoon it (1 teaspoon) into juice for an internal anaesthetic. Be aware that propolys is a natural antibiotic. Research shows that propolys changes the outer proteinaceous membrane of viruses, inhibiting their ability to dissolve the outer protective wall of the cell membrane. Propolys is nature's healing anaesthetic and is in its own right a plant hormone. It can act like a steroid, reducing inflammation. Burns treated with a propolys spray provides ease, reduces inflammation, and helps keep the cells free of microorganisms. Evidence may show in the future that the elements of propolys can biologically be transmutated in a manner that help the body heal. Propolys can help heal ulcers and in bronchial conditions to breathe easier. Propolys is a remarkably effective substance for helping the body heal fungal infections.

A NOTE TO THE SUGAR-SENSITIVE PERSON

Sugar-sensitive people can benefit from the use of flax meal and cinnamon to help slow the release of sugar into the body (bloodstream). Stir several heaping tablespoons of freshly ground flax seed into fresh raw juices or sprinkle over fruit meals. Also, ½–1 teaspoon of ground cinnamon, 2 or 3 times daily, helps to slow the release of sugar into the bloodstream, making the energy gained from the sugar become available more evenly and consistently.

A NOTE ABOUT FRECKLES

Freckles result when refined sugar in the bloodstream is drawn to the surface epidermal via the strong yang energy of the sun. Cut out refined sugar and watch the freckles disappear! Also, a LifeFood diet rich in enzymes will allow you to take more sunshine at a time and tan evenly and well. Liver flushes are greatly indicated here. Several 14-Day Fasts will start to turn the situation around. An abundance of dark leafy organic greens, particularly bitter greens like dandelion, act as a tonic to reduce freckles.

THE NIGHTSHADES

Members of the nightshade family include eggplant, peppers, tomatoes, potatoes, bell peppers, and tobacco.

Nightshades contain solanine, which can be a major factor for the arthritic person. Ireland (potato lovers) and Italy (tomato lovers) have the highest incidence of arthritis. We have a few recipes included here that contain tomatoes (use only vine ripened, organic) and peppers. Use them sparingly, or eliminate them for 2 weeks if you have arthritis and see if symptoms are relieved. Certain types of arthritis have been known to be greatly relieved simply by removing nightshades from the diet.

A NOTE ON PUMPKIN SEED & MELATONIN

Pumpkin seed has the amino acid tryptophane that is important in the hypothalamus production of the neurotransmitter serotonin. Serotonin is important in the ability to visualize and for sleep. It is a precursor substrate in the synthesis of the very important neurotransmitter/hormone called melatonin. Pumpkin seeds have the gene-repairing vitamin, Vitamin B17, amygdalin, essential fatty acids, and starch that can be broken down into simple sugars in the body. They also have anti-carcinogenic and anti-mutant properties. These essential fatty acids are extremely beneficial in healing conditions of the heart.

Melatonin is an important neuro-chemical that is involved in regulating all of the body's diurnal cycles. The importance of melatonin can be easily gauged because it is in the center of the nucleus of every cell of the body. The nucleus of the cell is where information is stored and used for the manufacture of specific proteins. These proteins support of all of our psycho-physiological processes and our characteristic shape and form. Pumpkin seeds are a tasty way to deliver these important nutrients.

pH (PARTS OF HYDROGEN)

Body pH is to your body what a blank canvas is to a painter. It is the background chemistry of life. Enzymes are involved in every biological reaction in the body. Enzymes require a specific pH. Enzymes are so important that breathing, digesting, and the other metabolic processes, like energy production within the mitochondria of the cells, can only occur with enzymes. Body pH has to be in balance for enzymes to function properly.

Your digestion is a key to any therapy. The enzymes in saliva and digestive fluids depend upon the body, pH balance to work correctly. An alkaline ash of what we drink and eat is what is left over after things are combusted at some level. Eating LifeFood, drinking alkaline water, and taking whole food vitamin supplements should balance body pH.

Electricity in your body is pH sensitive. pH in your body is the medium of this electricity that creates a living body for the very same reason that when a battery has electricity it is more alkaline and as it becomes dead it becomes more acidic. Body pH is a medium to the body, allowing it to act like a wet cell battery. This all starts by having the proper intestinal flora.

Your brain depends on oxygen and glucose and amino acid delivery to brain cells. Body pH is vital in this process. The autonomic nervous system and hormones, the electrical potential on the inside of your gut and the outside wall, is integral for any assimilation to take place. Everything is pH sensitive.

Vitality is about having a good body pH as is reflected in urine and saliva pH in the range of 6.8 to 7.0. It is a reflection of the body's vital immune system and ability to resist degenerative conditions. The Standard American Diet (SAD) is extremely acid-forming in the body. Virtually all cooked starches and all denatured food is acid-forming in the body, while LifeFood is alkaline-forming and brings about a pH balance. We pay special attention to this balance because most people living in the modern world are extremely acidic. We need to flood the body with usable nutrition that is highly alkaline and can rinse waste acids from the body. Acids tend to accumulate with age and that's why the most dramatic results from a LifeFood diet often come from older people. Joints and back stiffness are relieved and mental clarity is sharpened when the body pH comes into a natural balance.

FINAL WORD

It was Thomas Jefferson who said that the doctors of the future would educate people on how to care for their own health. It is in this spirit that we wrote this book and do all of our work—to bring to you the tools for building health so as to empower you, your family, and the human family at large.

Most aberrant behavior that we see around us in the world, such as crime and violence, can be corrected or greatly affected through proper nutrition. This was dramatically demonstrated when staff and teachers at Central Alternative High School in Appleton, Wisconsin, took action against the violence, gun-toting, wise-cracking, and truancy that had become regular behavior among the students. In 1997, they challenged the system and changed the menu at the cafeteria, and removed all the candy and soda vending machines. The cafeteria switched from offering hamburgers, hotdogs, french fries, cookies, cakes, chips, and soda to offering wholesome fresh fruit and vegetables, hormone-free eggs, cheese, and meat. They cut out all food containing the preservatives BHA, BHT, TBHQ, and synthetic colors and flavors. They started preparing meals using old-fashioned recipes. Principal LuAnn Coenen now files stunning figures each year with the state of Wisconsin. Since 1997, she has reported a figure of zero for drop-outs, student expulsion, and for students discovered using drugs, carrying weapons, and committing suicide. Zero. These problem behaviors simply disappeared when a wholesome diet was introduced and the worst chemical additives were removed. Now that daily discipline issues from chem'd-out kids isn't taking away from the teachers' time and attention, they report that the rewards of teaching have increased dramatically. One teacher who had been looking forward to retirement decided to put it off for another few years. He was having too much fun teaching these great kids. One student summed it up, "Now that I can concentrate, I think it's easier to get along with people."

The Earth came to us as a gift from our ancestors and it is on loan to us from our children. Native American wisdom teaches us that each generation is responsible to the seven generations that come after it. As upright and responsible people we can keep an eye out for each generation as it comes up behind us. Through our daily habits we can powerfully enhance the quality of life for ourselves, our neighbors that we share the planet with, all creatures great and small, the forests, and the waterways. And you'll be doing your most important task: to be the best person that you can be, for the good of all sentient beings, and to fulfill your sacred promise to the seventh generation.

RESOURCES

Jubbs Longevity, Inc. is a retail store for all Jubb recommended products. Visit or mail order: books, whole food vitamin/mineral supplements and LifeFood fasting products, dehydrated treats, gourmet LifeFood patisserie, LifeFood beverages, air and water filters, juicers, dehydrators, finest exotic oil, and all recommended products by Annie Jubb and Dr. David Jubb.

ORDER LIFEFOOD PRODUCTS

Jubbs LONGEVITY, INC.
508 East 12th Street
New York City, NY 10009

Phone: 212.353.5000

www.LifeFood.com & www.jubbslongvevity.com

NOTES

1. Center for Disease Control, October 2002 report.

2. California Center for Public Health Advocacy, www.publichealthadvocacy.org.

3. *Los Angeles Times*. November 30, 2002. By Ellen Ruppel Shell. Big food has become a big problem.

4. Rudgers University study.

5. Annie Padden Jubb & David Jubb, Ph.D. *Colloidal Biology and Secrets of an Alkaline Body* (self-published, 1993).

6. Louis Kervran. *Biological Transmutation* (Binghamton, NY: Swan House, 1972).

7. EarthSave materials (www.earthsave.com).

8. This study, focusing on toxic chemicals in the blood, was done by the federal Centers for Disease Control and Prevention.

9. www.seedsofchange.com.

10. From Michael Pollan's article in *The New York Times:* "When a Crop Becomes King," July 19, 2002. Many helpful facts were taken from his article to help write this chapter. He is also the author of *The Botany of Desire: A Plant's-Eye View of the World* (New York: Random House, 2002).

11. California Center for Public Health Advocacy (www.publichealthadvocacy.org).

12. U.S. Department of Agriculture.

INDEX

ABOUT THE AUTHORS

ANNIE PADDEN JUBB

Born in Seattle and raised on Guemes Island in Washington State, Annie moved to New York City in her late teens to study and teach intrinsic properties of health. She has owned and managed raw organic vegan restaurants in San Francisco and Hawaii, and currently in New York City's East Village and Los Angeles. She lives in Los Angeles, providing health readings to clients and overseeing fasts, running corporate workshops, writing and filming, and conducting health research.

DAVID JUBB, Ph.D.

Born and raised on a remote island in Tasmania, Australia, David journeyed to the U.S. to study, receiving his doctorate at New York University. He took 2 years off to trek the entire length of Africa. An Exercise and Behavior Physiologist, he has devoted the latter part of his career to the anatomy of health. His Health Readings are sought out the world over, as he is renowned for his accuracy in pinpointing the origin of a symptom and how to heal it naturally. David currently maintains a busy private practice in New York City and is always writing and lecturing, both in the U.S. and abroad.

Annie Jubb and Dr. David Jubb have authored nine books together, including *Secrets to an Alkaline Body: The New Science of Colloidal Biology, Shamanism: The Path of Formlessness,* and *Cell Rejuvenation,* along with five training manuals for their Whole Brain Functioning adventure-based learning program taught at retreats and lectures throughout the 1980s and '90s. They have had a weekly TV show in Manhattan since 1998. Jubbs LifeFood Nutritional Fasting Outpatient Clinic, established in 1990, continues to help many thousands each year to safely detoxify, tissue cleanse, and restore good health in the body. The Jubbs maintain private practices in New York City and Los Angeles.

Jubbs LONGEVITY, Inc. is a retail store for all Jubb-recommended products for diet, personal grooming, and home. Enjoy the LifeFood Beverage Bar and gourmet LifeFood Patisserie. When in New York, stop in to pick up everything you need to equip your LifeFood kitchen, purify your tap water for drinking and bathing, and stock up on living whole food vitamins, super foods, and LifeFood treats.

Call for a catalog

Jubbs LONGEVITY, INC.
508 East 12th Street
New York City, NY 10009

Phone: 212.353.5000

www.LifeFood.com & www.jubbslongvevity.com